POWER: A REPOSSESSION MANUAL

organizing strategies for citizens
by Greg Speeter
of the Citizen Involvement Training
Project (CITP)

The Citizen Involvement Training Project (CITP) is a collaborative project of the Division of Continuing Education and the Cooperative Extension Service at the University of Massachusetts at Amherst. CITP is funded by a major grant from the W. K. Kellogg Foundation of Battle Creek, Michigan, with additional support from the Blanchard and Polaroid Foundations.

Our thanks to the reviewers of this manual:

- Carlos Vega, Holyoke Mass Fair Share, Holyoke, Mass.
- Reene Romano, Brightwood Neighborhood Council, Springfield, Mass.
- Joe Roche, Planning Director, Western Massachusetts Health Planning Council, West Springfield, Mass.
- Dean Hudson, Citizen Involvement Training Project, Amherst, Mass.
- Susan Kohler, Massachusetts Public Interest Research Group, Amherst, Mass.
- Betsy D. Klare, Department of Mental Health, Springfield, Mass.

© **University of Massachusetts (Citizen Involvement Training Project) 1978**

The contents of this manual are the sole responsibility of the authors; endorsement of the content by the University of Massachusetts or sponsoring organizations should not be inferred.

Cover photos: Lionel Delevingne

Acknowledgments

A number of people deserve credit for helping me with this manual. I'd like to thank **Dean Hudson**, intern at CITP, for his insightful review of the entire manual, for his encouragement, and for helping to make the first chapter coherent; **Dave Magnani**, CITP Director, for supplying his analysis, vision, and for allowing himself to be interrupted continually to comment on various sections during the last few weeks of the unit process; to the rest of the **CITP staff** for ideas and comments.

Thanks also to the reviewers, for helpful ideas and suggestions; the **Word Processing Center** and the **Division of Continuing Education** for typing, typesetting, and organizational support; participants in my organizing workshops, who came up with many of the ideas for the content of the manual; and to **Betsy** and **Beth** for putting up with my craziness over the past three months.

I couldn't have written this manual unless I was convinced beyond a doubt that community organizing works, and if any people made me realize that, it was the people in the North End of Springfield, Massachusetts, who, in 1968 and 1969, set up the **Spanish American Union**. Thanks Christine, Juan, Dorothy, Peter, Gregorio, Victor, Wilfredo and William, Ildephonso, Tom, Dot, Frank, Barbara, Yvette, Angel and many others in the North End for (literally) demonstrating to the city of Springfield and me that by being dedicated to a vision, we can conquer windmills, slumlords, repressive police, and stubborn bureaucrats.

ISBN 0-934210-00-4
Library of Congress
Catalog Card Number: 79-624732

1st printing, November 1978
2nd printing, July, 1979
3rd printing, March, 1980

Contributing Photographers:

Jennifer Cobb
Sarah Deering
Lionel Delevingne
Kayla Kirsch
Mark Ross

Contributing Artists:

Meg Davenport
Wayne Friedrich
Lorie Leininger
Ann McCaffrey
Brian Turner

(plus numerous photos and artwork from the CPF--Community Press Features--files.)

Paste-up:

Patricia Cahill
Robbie Gordon
Miriam Leader
Terry Mathison
Maureen O'Brian

Stats:

Terry Mathison

Typesetting:

Division of Continuing Education Publications Department; University of Massachusetts/Amherst

Our thanks to the Valley Advocate for the use of several photos and articles from their files.

Manual Design/Layout:

Robbie Gordon

Editing:

Robbie Gordon
Ken Walker

TABLE OF CONTENTS

Acknowledgements i

Introduction 1

    How to Use This Manual 3
    About the Exercises 3
    About the Use of "He," "She" 3
    About the Use of the Word "Organizer" 3
    Some Methods of Developing an Organizer's Culture 4

Chapter I: Developing Your Own Theory of Community Organizing 5

    Questions to Ask of Your Community:
        1. The Real Situation 7
        2. Vision 8
        3. Analysis 9
        4. Strategies 10
    The Need for a Theory 11
    Some Social Change Strategies 12
    Approaches to Organizing 16
    The Organizer as Person 21
    Steps Involved in Community Organizing 21

Chapter II: Identifying Issues 23

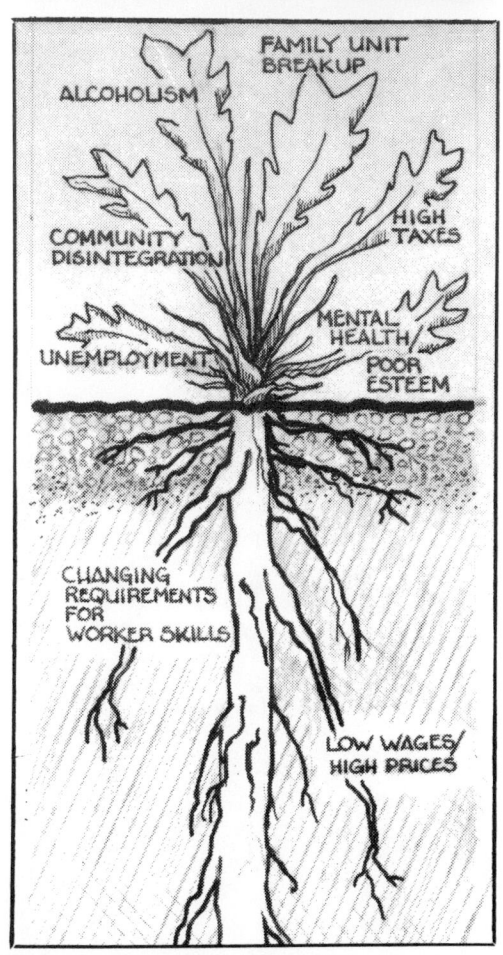

    Various Approaches 26
    Am I Prepared to Organize? 29
    Have I Spent Time in the Community? 33
    Information Gathering Techniques 34
    Developing Trust 36
    Identifying the Issues: Mapping a Strategy 37
    Gathering Information Exercises 38
    Ways to Prioritize Problems 44
    Have We Decided on an Issue? 45
    Identifying Root Causes 47
    How to Get to the Root of the Problem 49

    Root Causes: A Few Assumptions........................ 50

    Root Cause Questions to Ask of Yourself and Your Group.... 54

Chapter III: How Structure Develops Power.. 57

    Discussion: The Role of Structure in Organizing............ 61

    For the Organizers: Typical Hassles in Developing Structure... 63

    Approaches to Developing Structure..................... 66

    Utilizing Resources................................. 68

    Risk-Taking in Working for Social Change................ 72

    Seven Ways to Build Community Leadership.............. 75

    Group Decision-Making: Means to an End................ 76

    A Way to Improve the Decision-Making Process........... 78

Chapter IV: Taking Action....................... 79

    Case Histories..................................... 79

    What Organizations Get from Action.................... 81

    Possible Problems.................................. 82

    Action: Various Approaches........................... 84

    Vision: A Social Change Perspective.................... 86

    Matching Action with Levels of Resistance............... 88

    Strategy Checklists:

        Collaborative Strategies........................ 92

        Campaign Strategies........................... 97

        Confrontation Strategies....................... 101

    Tactics in Organizing................................ 108

    Role-Playing: A "Rehearsal" for Action.................. 109

    Role-Play Scenario #1............................... 111

    Role-Play Scenario #2............................... 114

Chapter V: Evaluation and Future Directions 115

Resources.. 117

    Newsletters.. 117

    Films.. 117

    Books... 118

    Handbooks... 121

1

INTRO-
DUCTION

The problem with those of us who have been involved in organizing is, *we ain't got no culture.* Oh, we've got just about everything else. Take our ability to be significant. The roles which community organizations played in the civil rights movement, the anti-war movement, the women's movement and the war on poverty (to name just a few) make us probably the most significant approach to social change in the past 20 years. The tactics we used, the long hours we spent, the continued demand to "let the people take charge" all testify to our zany cleverness, our dedication and our idealism.

Unfortunately, we don't share this with each other—we don't *develop* our culture. *We don't talk out our organizing with each other, we just go on to organize around other issues* (confrontation junkies, all).

Lionel Delevingne

The most dramatic example of this is the lack of real written material on the subject of organizing. If, as I've said, we took major responsibility for significant social changes, how come we haven't published all the books and periodicals and TV shows that educators, the mental health and health professions have published? It is virtually impossible to walk into your local library and pick up a book which describes the best tactics to use in winning a rent strike, or discusses ways to stop a nuclear power plant or forces rich people to pay taxes, even though community organizations have been working in these areas for years. You'll have to search hard and long to find now to organize to hold a TV station accountable to FCC regulations, how students can start their own school or how to set up a community-run economic development corporation.

Isolated from each other, we develop an arrogance and type of independence that has kept us from learning from each other, and from developing coalitions with each other's groups.

But even when one has found information on organizing, much of it is written just for the professional organizer, not for all those community people who make up the organization. Organizers have claimed to want to "work ourselves out of jobs," yet we still tend to use skills on people rather than share skills with people.

HOW TO USE THIS MANUAL

This manual is written to encourage the growth of a culture of community organization and to make the process of mobilizing a community and the skills involved known to all those who will be a part of an organizing process. Like the community organizing process itself, this manual is based on experience (including your experience) and active involvement in the learning process. Essentially, this manual consists of ways to understand your own organizing process, to diagnose it and to prescribe ways to improve it.

This book is written with the assumption that *group members (not group leaders)* should own the organization (its actions, programs and decisions). Though the book addresses itself often to the "organizer(s)," it is hoped that those who start the organization will share the information with new members as a way of strengthening and developing membership.

Chapters are written chronologically, from the first step in the organizing process through the last. Each step (chapter) is divided into a series of methods or substeps which usually are required to accomplish a step. (For instance, in order to determine an issue in step one, we need to talk with people, do research, evaluate and prioritize issues, etc.) You may, however, want to use these sections as if they were modules and regroup the modules according to your needs.

ABOUT THE EXERCISES

There are several exercises and sections in this manual which you might want to duplicate, reorder to suit your group's needs or use as a smaller, condensed version of a "training workbook" for the entire group.

Whatever way you use the manual, we hope you will tailor it to suit your own needs and learning styles. All exercises in the manual have been formatted on single pages so that you can duplicate them easily; exercises are denoted as such so that you will know they are optional as you read through each chapter. You may want to read through the entire body of the manual before trying the exercises. On the other hand, many people find that the information in the manual has more relevance after they do the exercises.

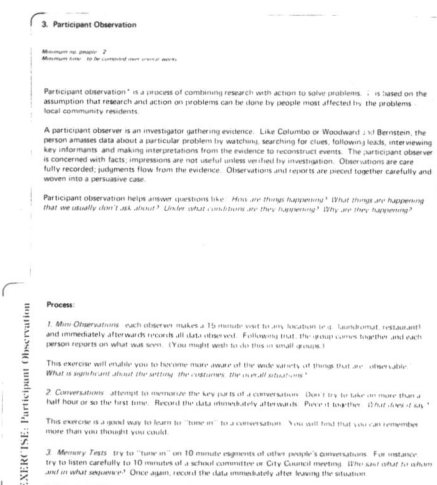

ABOUT THE USE OF "HE", "SHE"... etc.

In an effort to overcome the inherent male bias in our English language, the producers of this manual have run up against the cumbersome problem of having to break up the flow of a sentence or train of thought by saying he/she, him/herself, etc. We have, therefore, decided to alternate the use of the personal pronoun throughout the body of the manual: sometimes we call the organizer he, sometimes she. This is not a stylistic mistake, it was purposeful. It is hoped that our culture will devise appropriate pronouns in the future to compensate for the problems currently presented authors and editors (not to mention men and women).

ABOUT THE USE OF THE WORD 'ORGANIZER'

This book is primarily geared toward those persons interested in organizing a community or group of people around a social change issue and for those people who "get organized" or mobilized. Unfortunately, the word "organizer" generally tends to imply one sort of organizer—the community organizer. We hope that any person(s) who wish to become social-change agents will be able to apply the contents of this manual to their own situation...whether they are paid/professional organizers, part time volunteers, or one-time-only activists. We also hope that those who initially take the leadership initiative will share this manual with all the members of her group so that the entire membership is

aware of the process necessary to mobilize a group of people, and can participate more effectively in the process.

SOME METHODS OF DEVELOPING AN ORGANIZER'S CULTURE

People learn in different ways. This manual provides a number of different ways for people to learn and diagnose their learning needs, through:

• **"trigger" questions:** questions that you may not normally ask yourself which will hopefully trigger food for thought;

• **planning questions**, to help you figure out your next steps;

• **role-play situations**, to help you come up with some data on yourself and to help you practice certain kinds of behaviors and responses to situations;

• **diagnostic criteria**, to help you determine whether there have been some aspects of a situation you may have neglected to look at;

• **case studies**; ways to learn from other people's successes and failures;

• **information and skill sharing**;

• **famous quotations** (we *do* need culture).

CITP files

It is difficult to try to write a manual about a process as organic and constantly changing as organizing for social change. We have attempted to collect here whatever information already exists on the subject with our own experience and models. We realize, however, that there are as many different approaches as there are personalities, and so we'd like to ask you to help us complete this book.

In several places we have left lists incomplete, for you to add your own ideas and experiences. We would appreciate your sharing these with us, to help us build that culture we spoke of earlier.

CHAPTER I: DEVELOPING YOUR OWN THEORY OF COMMUNITY ORGANIZING

Taking the time to read a manual on organizing is probably a luxury for most people involved in social change—you've probably got another meeting to plan for tomorrow or your crisis has you constantly *reacting* to one event after another, which allows you little time for *acting consciously*.

As people who work with others in your community, it is often easy to become caught up in the immediate day-to-day struggles with which we are involved. These can take on such extreme importance that we often lose sight of our larger vision of the kind of society and quality of life we are attempting to realize through the organizing process—a vision that probably originally played a central role in motivating us to become involved in the organizing process. This first section is an attempt to stimulate your thinking on the important question of what organizing is all about. It poses some very basic questions:

• *What things do you see in the present society which you feel need changing?*

• *What would society look like if these changes could be brought about?*

• *What kinds of obstacles prevent us from realizing them?*

• *Given these obstacles, what kinds of strategies of community organizing and social change can we develop and use to overcome them?*

From these four questions you should be able to develop your own theory, on which you can base future organizing.

It is obviously quite beyond the scope of this manual to offer any conclusive resolution to these various complex questions. Our intent here is simply to suggest some guidelines and questions concerning the kinds of things one might take into consideration when developing a social analysis and theory of change, and to present some very brief sketches of the kinds of answers others have come up with when considering these issues.

So, even if you do have a committee meeting to plan for next Monday, why not play with these questions first? The answers you finally arrive at, even if only tentative, can greatly influence your whole approach to the organizing process—what kinds of projects you will work on, what kinds of strategies and tactics you will use, who you will turn to for support, what kinds of compromises you will find acceptable. Some of the best organizers I know feel that periodic struggling with the basic questions helps put those everyday hassles into perspective and helps develop a critical consciousness of the world and our work.

One way of thinking about questions concerning social analysis and strategies of social change is outlined below. Four basic areas are to be taken into consideration:

• *the real situation in your community;*

• *your vision of the kind of community you would like to live in (the kinds of changes you would like to bring about through the organizing process);*

• *an analysis of those persons, forces, and structures which currently prevent your vision from being realized;*

• *the kinds of strategies, tactics and structures that could be used to overcome the social and political obstacles which prevent you from reaching your goal.*

Following are some questions that one might ask when reflecting on these four areas. They can be used as guidelines in the exploration and development of your own theory of social analysis and social change.

Listed to the right on each of these four questions is an example of how a Holyoke, Massachusetts, resident who is about to become active in a community organizing process answered these questions.

"You see what is and ask, 'why?' I see what could be and ask, 'why not?'"
—George Bernard Shaw

You may want to respond to these questions in general, or pick a specific concern of yours in the community, and relate the questions to that specific concern, as our Holyoke friend did in the example below.

1. THE REAL SITUATION:
What needs changing in the community?

Questions

1. Do you feel that all people's basic needs are presently being met in your community?

Are people's needs being met in terms of:

- education?
- access to meaningful and rewarding work?
- easy access to sensible and inexpensive transportation?
- a healthy diet? *NO* *Pro cathedral St. Andrews, Santa Fund.*
- adequate medical care and preventive health care? *NO.*

2. How much say or influence do you feel the people in your community have over these areas as they affect their lives?

don't feel they have an awful lot of say. They are in

many cases unaware. Always feel it is their fault. Aged, teen moms etc. eg. those in infant stim. program.

Interview

While this interview deals with employment, an issue most community organizers are unable to deal with, it was chosen because it is an issue that is central to the hearts of people in most every community, and offers the direction in which many community organizations could go.

"Well, for most of us in Holyoke, a lot of our needs aren't being met, but perhaps the area that really affects most of us is employment. The Department of Employment Security says that the rate of unemployment is about 10% here, but that only includes those who have recently signed up at DES. So it doesn't include people like my cousin, who has given up on going to DES because he hasn't been able to get a job in the year he's been going down there...same old story for him...'Sorry, no jobs in your field today.' You see, Holyoke's lost a lot of business in the past 15 years. Like a lot of towns in New England, we're dying out.

"There are also people not included in that 10% figure—underemployed—like my father, still making under $10,000 as a chef in a city where people can no longer afford to go out to eat.

"Then there are people like myself—working in a factory like at least half the people in the city, but not really enjoying it. The wages are mediocre, and the jobs are boring.

"Just drive through the lower wards of Holyoke and look at the deteriorated housing and empty warehouses, or talk to some kids in school.

"I help make checkbooks, but do you think I'll ever have enough money to write checks other than for immediate necessities? It seems we all make things we never use.

"The other thing I didn't talk about much regarding work is the competition. Affirmative Action wouldn't bother me a bit if I knew we'd all have jobs."

We all have a vision of our ideal community or ideal society, even if it's a pipe dream, and even if there are contradictions to that vision. As someone involved in community organizing, you'll be helping yourself and others attain power to meet their needs. Since your work reflects your concern about community, power, control, the quality of human relations, your particular vision of what should be changed in the community and the end product of that change will greatly influence the kinds of community organizing projects you will engage in and towards what ends they will be directed.

2. VISION: What would the ideal community/society look like?

[handwritten margin note: much communication with community]

Questions

1. Should some people direct and control others? (If yes, how could that control be implemented? On what basis could that exercise of control be legitimized?) *[handwritten: Collective control decision making. idealistic]*

2. How could decision-making take place in this community?

3. How could resources be allocated?

4. How could people relate to each other (especially men and women, minorities and whites, young and old)? *[handwritten: more aware of each other]*

5. What kinds of access should people have to their government?

6. What kinds of control should people have over their work life? How could the quality of work life be improved? *[handwritten: Ch. 10 BTV]*

7. What kinds of economic structures would you envision that would allow this kind of change in the quality of work life?

8. How could people's educational, recreational and health needs be met? *[handwritten: Community health services & subsidies]*

9. How do you envision people's relationship to nature?

Interview

"Let's take the work situation again. Some people quit their jobs because they were terrible jobs. You know, long hours, low wages, dangerous, stressful.

"Ideally, I'd like to find a way where workers couldn't be exploited by management. Some people in our union have been talking a lot about places where workers own their own plant. They share in the way things get done, and also share in the profits.

"One thing I'd like about that is that we could decide to make useful products that the ordinary family needs—home insulation and inexpensive heating; good, chemical-free food; inexpensive housing. It would really boost my spirits to make something I knew people needed and enjoyed."

Donn Young, Valley Advocate

The kinds of changes that you would like to see occur in your present community would probably be supported by a great many people, since those changes would bring about a vast improvement in the quality of life. What kinds of obstacles would prevent members of your community from collectively realizing their vision?

3. ANAYLSIS: Why is there a gap between the real and the ideal?

Questions

1. Does the problem lie in the political power and decision-making structure?

2. Does it lie in access to economic power and decision-making?

3. Is it due to unwieldy social and political structures whose enormous size keeps them from changing?

4. Who gains from the situation?

5. How do they gain?

6. Who loses from the situation?

7. How do they lose?

Modern Times/cpf

Interview

"There is no doubt in my mind that the reason for the difference between what is really going on in Holyoke and what I want to happen in Holyoke is that those who own the industries are more concerned about profits than they are about people. Like I've said before, we've lost a lot of industry in our town. Even our mayor has said we've lost 25% of our taxable income in the last few years because industry finds it cheaper to move down south or overseas rather than stay here. We have no say whether business stays or goes, to say nothing about having a say over what we make or how we make it.

"But the problem is more complicated than that. The city government may try to offer tax breaks to new industry—which means our property tax goes up, and our taxes are already among the top 5% in the country. So even if we do get business in, taxes won't go down.

"Our union hasn't had much say in these kinds of issues. We've been concerned about getting more money, pensions, safety and vacations. Maybe we should have been concerned about these larger issues too, but you can only do so much.

"The best way to really understand what's going on in the community is to ask who gains and who loses from our job situation.

"Obviously the management and the big stockholders gain from this. But the guy who is always afraid that his job will go—loses out. In the competition between black and white, men and women, young workers and older workers, both sides lose, because we blame each other."

10 Now we come to perhaps the most important questions for the community organizer. Yet the answers one comes up with here will depend on the kinds of answers one reaches concerning the previous questions.

Below are listed some questions to help you develop your own strategy, as well as the answers our friend from Holyoke gave for his strategy. Following that are listed a few of the many strategies, tactics, approaches and structures which some political and economic "theorists" have suggested for addressing the problems we have addressed here.

Sarah Deering

4. STRATEGY:
What strategies can be developed to work toward solving the problem?

Questions

1. How can we as organizers and members of a community go about overcoming the obstacles which prevent us from realizing the quality of life which we envision?

2. What actions can we use to confront the problems and obstacles we have outlined in our analysis of the existing situation?

3. What kinds of organizational, social and political structures can be used—not only to confront the existing situation, but also the kinds of structures that could be used to implement and maintain the kind of life which you envision could exist in your community?

4. Who should be involved in the struggle?

5. What groups or individuals could be counted on for support?

6. How will you know when you're winning?

7. How will you know when you've won?

Interview

"I'm most interested in developing a worker-controlled business. I guess one way to begin is to talk about the problems and my vision with others who see it my way, or could see it my way. Together we could bring it up at our union. Unions in general could gain from workers owning their own plants.

"Then we'd certainly want to find where this type of action has gone on in the past, to learn from its mistakes and successes.

"I imagine we could probably get the support and resources of some elected officials. They could support us and pass legislation that would be favorable to worker control.

"Now that I think of it, the list of supporters is growing—churches, community groups, the food co-op..."

THE NEED FOR A THEORY

Probably the biggest problem people who want to bring about social change face is, *where to begin?* It's the one problem that makes most people back off. Those who see problems with the system often go running off to stick their thumbs in one hole in the dike, only to find another leak in a spot they can't reach (and still keep the other hole plugged).

Some people try to bring about change by working on immediate problems (social service agencies, drug and mental health clinics); some treat the individual (psychologists and social workers, physicians, job counselors); some try to work on society as a whole (sociologists, political theorists, policy analysts, public administrators); some work on one particular aspect of society (environmentalists, educators, health care reformers, welfare and tenants rights activists). The frustration that each faces, however, is that working for social change is like untying a series of knots—some knots can't even be gotten to until others are untied first. (How can you mobilize people around an issue when protesting involves questioning authority, and an individual's belief in authority has everything to do with their personal sense of self-esteem, life values and need for security?)

The question is, what makes people change and, where can you personally put your energies, skills and talents to help most effectively untie some of those knots?

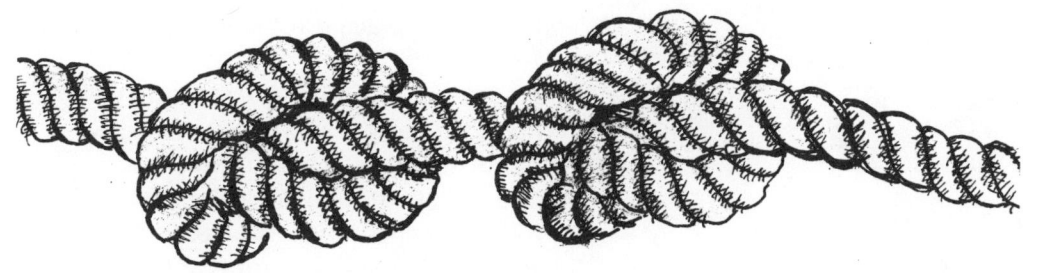

Wayne Friedrich

"...working for social change is like untying a series of knots--some knots can't even be reached until others are untied first."

At this point it becomes clear that social change agents need to have some sort of theory of social change which guides their actions and efforts. Even before one sets about deciding on a set of goals for an organization (for example, to eliminate sexism in education), one first has to have a theory about how change will occur as a guide in setting those goals (public education and educational reform can change basic problems with the system).

The following are a few social change theories which you may want to consider before sitting down and defining (or refining) your own. Whether or not you agree with the theories, they can help provide models to trigger thought, disagreement and new ideas. Your own theory may be a combination of elements from each theory (and others); or you may have a totally different point of view. Regardless, it will be helpful for you to ask yourself what your basic assumptions are about people, social change and the present political/social/economic system.

Political economists and social change theorists are increasingly identifying the unjust economic structure as a basic or root cause of most social problems. In a nutshell, they see that major corporations go after more and more profits, either by expanding production and distribution, or by increasing profit margins per unit produced. The first method requires market expansion (to the whole world, eventually), and the production of useless or destructive goods, of which our friend from Holyoke spoke. The other method of increasing profit has resulted in unemployment increases through automation and speed-ups. As unemployment increases, wages are kept down. And as real wages go down, production must go higher or prices go higher just to keep profits at the same rate. Under this, the worker cannot save, and ultimately he cannot buy as much. Goods go unsold, and so production is slowed and unemployment increases. Ultimately, the system collapses under the weight of its own progress.

Instead of a worker's revolution, however, we find a depression. Why? These theorists believe that the government operates to curb the excesses of capitalism in order to save it. The "collective will" of the corporate executives allows certain "socialist mechanisms" in order to blunt worker consciousness and appease discontent. Thus we find unemployment compensation, welfare, wage and price controls and the like.

What response--what strategy--should people make to this situation? The following are some capsule strategies of a few social theorists.

SOME SOCIAL CHANGE STRATEGIES

1. Worker Control — Organize People as Workers

Writer Andre Gorz puts his emphasis on the worker, saying that real equality in society will not take place until workers cooperatively own the means of production. For Gorz, change will not come through evolution, but through revolution, a critical "trial of strength," won by workers, followed by a continual critical analysis of the changes that have occurred, to insure that the old forms will not reappear and new forms disintegrate.

A major step towards this "critical trial" is the winning or establishing of centers of democratic cooperative management in the major industries. Gorz calls for the building of a politically mature working class with skills and awareness for the development of political and managerial power before and after the trial of strength. This is necessary so that an institutional framework will exist, controlled by the workers, that can control the chain reaction of changes that the trial of strength will bring about.

Gorz is careful to distinguish between "reformist reform" and "revolutionary reform." He says that reformist reform only asks for more bread from the table, but does not ask for real control of the

Industrial Worker, Mar. 23, 1911

Donn Young, Valley Advocate

oven. Even if one requests a lot of bread, it does not change the eventual future condition of hunger, nor the future need to bake. A revolutionary reform, however, is one which brings about structural changes in power relations, even if they may not seem extreme (for example, workers represented on boards of directors, even if they are initially only in the minority). Gorz clearly advocates the latter type of reform.

2. Escalating Demands, Developing Coalitions

Another school of thought feels that while activity must take place within the labor movement, significant roles can be played in electoral politics and other social service institutions, as ways to increase appeasement or "mollification" programs. This leaves capitalists with the choice of either eliminating the programs (resulting in rebellion) or expansion of the programs. Program expansions raise expectations, calling forth more demands for more programs, and at least short-run victories. This group of theorists believes that demands will eventually rise to the point where they can only be satisfied by a worker's revolution, which need not involve serious violent opposition from the already beleagured agents of capital.

Through electoral politics (according to this theory), workers can battle racism and sexism, support graduated income tax, eliminate tax shelters, reduce hours in the work week, and cut back the arms race.

In addition, workers would develop important coalitions with other social service and educational institutions, as all these groups gain more from the "appeasement" programs.

3. Accountability — Organize People as Consumers

A movement that is less than 15 years old, but has developed considerable strength is the consumer movement, inspired most notably by Ralph Nader. This strategy by and large sees people as consumers (instead of workers) and attempts to encourage people to be satisfied consumers: be they consumers of products, of services, or of government.

Nader has been quick to show how corporations have tricked, deceived and robbed the American people, and has shown how the government has been an active accomplice in this. His research has played a major part in destroying the myths of the benevolent corporate elite, modifying its greed in order to produce goods to serve the people.

Kayla Kirsch/Jennifer Cobb

Nader, his affiliated Public Interest Research Groups (PIRG) across the country and similar organizations attempt to hold corporations, elected officials, the government bureaucracy and regulatory agencies accountable to the public. Emphasis is on people fighting for legal rights in making corporations and government more responsive to the "public interest." Citizens can battle secrecy, special interests and a labyrinth of regulations and, in effect, make the system workable, through knowledge of laws, regulations and initiative.

D C Gazette/cp

4. Organize "Non-Participation and Alternative Programming

Non-violent activists recognize that power is inherent in practically all social and political relationships, and that it is necessary to wield power to maintain control. But non-violent activists also see this political power generated and maintained at least in part by those who are ruled—the ruled allowing themselves to be oppressed—therefore perpetuating the social order.

However, non-violent activists maintain that if people refuse to engage in activities which continue to generate and maintain the power of the rulers, the power virtually

disintegrates. Manufacturers can not engage in the process of production without the labor of their workers. Military leaders cannot engage in battle if they have no soldiers who are willing to fight. Political leaders can not implement their policies without the cooperation of the agencies of administration. The agencies of administration can not implement the policies of political leaders if the people who work in the agencies (from top administrators to the office staff) refuse to carry out their routine activities. In all the instances, the basis of the power of the powerholder is eroded.

While non-violent action has sometimes been criticized as being oriented towards disruption, it also has offered alternatives. One of the ways in which people can refuse to cooperate with enterprises or organizations is to provide alternative structures, organized on different principles, through which those needs can be met. For instance, not only can workers refuse to cooperate

with their employer on a temporary basis (as in a strike), but they can also refuse to participate in the entire process of selling their labor to their employers. Instead they can employ themselves in the form of a worker's collective, cooperatively owned and operated, as was suggested in the Holyoke example.

5. Freirian Approach — Awareness, Action, Reflection

Some, such as Paulo Freire, believe that conditions will not change unless those oppressed go *beyond conforming* to *reforming*; to seeing that the situation really requires transformation. Doing so, developing this "critical consciousness," helps people understand the political and economic contradictions in society.

Freire would bring together people who experience common oppressions. After some discussion and analysis, they would set up a program of action, followed by reflection on both the results of the action and what it teaches about the way the system operates and the laws of power within it. This understanding thus helps to focus future actions on those issues which most directly attack the roots of the problem, rather than the symptoms.

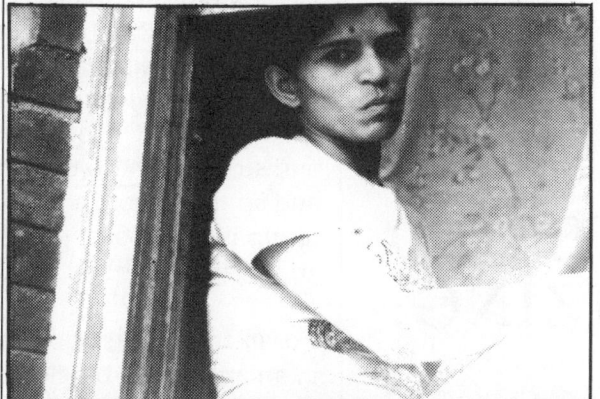
Kayla Kirsch/Jennifer Cobb

Kayla Kirsch/Jennifer Cobb

6. "Poor People's Movements" — Protest and Disrupt

In a book, **Poor Peoples' Movements, How They Succeed, Why They Fail,*** (a book all members of community organizations should read), authors Piven and Cloward maintain that both the possibilities and limitations of mass protest and change are shaped by social conditions. Protest is not created by organizers or leaders but is a response to momentous changes in the institutional order, brought about by *deprivation* (such as the Depression and southern economic transformation which forced blacks into cities), *disorganization* (because institutions can no longer regulate, routines are broken), and *demand for redress* (when poor no longer blame themselves for their plight, they may cause spontaneous disruption).

Once protest erupts, the specific forms it takes are largely determined by features of social structure. Organizers and leaders who contrive strategies that ignore the social location of the people they seek to mobilize can only fail. Whatever influence lower class groups occasionally exert in American politics does not result from organization, but from the mass protest and the disruptive consequences of protest.

Organizers and leaders cannot prevent the ebbing of protest nor the erosion of whatever influence protest yielded the lower class. They can only try to win whatever can be won while it can be won. According to Piven and Cloward, strategies must be pursued which escalate the momentum and impact of disruptive protest at each stage in its emergence and evolution.

Lionel Delevingne

***Poor Peoples' Movements—Why They Succeed, How They Fail,** by Frances Fox Piven and Richard A. Cloward, Pantheon Books, New York, 1977.

APPROACHES TO ORGANIZING:

WHICH ONE BEST SUITS MY STYLE?

While most organizers generally agree about the steps involved in organizing, there are many different approaches to achieve each step. Different assumptions about what kinds of power people can actually achieve, what kinds of issues they can work on, what kinds of structures, leadership models and decision-making models people should participate in and what kinds of actions people should use, make for a wide variety of models for community organization. Listed here are some of the major approaches organizers have used in recent years and some key questions that can help deal with the problems organizers might face while working with a certain approach.

Think about each of these as possible organizing approaches or pieces or organizing models for your own situation. As you read, be thinking about which approaches suit you best in terms of:

- the best way you relate to people;

- the organizing strengths you have;

- your political beliefs;

- what's available as organizing possibilities where you live (or would want to live).

Alinsky — Style Organizing:

Alinsky organizers build small "block clubs" to allow small groups of people to win small victories, then build neighborhood coalitions and congresses from these block clubs to allow larger groups of people to win larger victories. Many Alinsky organizers research problems and possible strategies and then try to set up initial victories for their groups. Once leadership and structure have been tested, and strengthened, and once the group is victorious, people go on to larger battles and successes.

For example, a group of tenants in an apartment block tried to set up meetings with their landlord to bring about better housing. The meetings proved futile until these tenants organized tenants in other apartment blocks that the landlord owned, and threatened a rent strike.

Perhaps the most popular approach to organizing, this military style has been set up to develop sufficient mass power to force municipal governments or businesses to change oppressive domination.

Some of the **strengths** of this form of organizing include:

- the ability to deal with immediate concerns;

- a high energy level among participants;

- successful use of confrontation tactics to win rent strikes, battles with city hall, city officials, municipal government, etc.;

- ability to develop grassroots leadership and participation.

Mandated Citizen Participation Organizing:

This approach maintains that citizens should tell the government what issues it should deal with, and that citizens should have a say in government policies. Established as a response to the activism and demand for participation during the 60s and early 70s, this process has been used most widely in human services, education, health and housing. The government agency usually hires a staff person (or persons) to work part or full-time with citizens, educating citizens to the problems the agency is dealing with and eliciting citizen support to advocate reform and/or organize to change the system. There has been an increasing demand that consumers (non-providers of services or actual consumers of services) have at least 51% membership on these boards.

If working properly, the possibilities of organizing for change within the structure are impressive indeed. Federal mandates allow for citizens to control millions of dollars in health care monies annually in the 200 health planning councils in the United States. In Massachusetts, state mandates allow students and parents to be able to determine possible educational curriculum and allow for students to meet periodically with school officials as well as allowing one student to participate as a member of the the State Board of Education. Some Councils for Children have organized citizens around significant children's issues. Many area councils and boards have regional and state boards as well to allow for participation on regional and state issues, and possibly to set up regional and state coalitions. There are currently *over 10,000* mandated boards in the state of Massachusetts alone.

The difference between advocating for reform vs. organizing for change is a crucial one here. Advocating for reform, often within certain guidelines (mandated by the government), may not allow citizens the real ability to define the issues themselves, and to develop themselves the most efficient and effective structure to solve the problems. Action in the form of confrontation is usually frowned upon. Real (as opposed to lip-service) organizing for citizen boards would allow citizens to hire/fire the organizer and determine the issues, the structure and the action, or it would provide an organizer who was willing to help the citizen board organize against the agency if necessary.

There are some **strengths** to this form of organizing. They include:

- serving as a "braking" mechanism to slow down the mistake-making ability of the system;

- acting as a consciousness-raising device, to show people what this system is really like;

- pinpointing government wastes and mismanagement;

- providing support for the notion of citizen participation (if we turn down this approach, we may lose a significant, though frustrating, way to influence the system).

Some of the **weaknesses** of this form of organizing include:

- lack of concern with consciousness raising (one of the most successful battles won by Alinsky managed to win jobs for blacks; however, the jobs were taken away from working class whites;

- it is often concerned almost exclusively with immediate problems, such as getting street lights put up on certain neighborhood corners; it is unclear what kind of strategy the group plans to develop to help people deal with issues more significant than street light level issues;

- organizers tend to manipulate situations to give people the appearance of power, when in fact it is the organizer that has the power.

The Free Press/cpf

Public Advocacy Organizing:

Some of the **weaknesses** of the approach include:

- providing "busy work" for citizens, instead of real organizing and advocacy power;

- increasing frustration from dealing with bureaucrats who don't want to listen to citizens;

- concentrating on symptoms of problems (such as drug abuse) instead of dealing with root causes (lack of roles for youth in the community, lack of meaningful jobs, etc.)

Here a small group of people decide on a basic issue, for a significant political-geographical area, such as a region of a state or an entire state, and tries to set up local groups to respond locally, and possibly coalesce regionally or state-wide to win an issue. Members are utilized to do research, to educate, to lobby, to initiate local actions and participate in larger actions. Members often act as representatives of other local groups, and a major function of the organizing can consist of coalition-building as oppsed to grassroots organizing.

When several of these groups work on the same issue in different geographical regions, the groups may share research, resources and strategies.

Some examples of this type of organizing include: The Mass. Public Interest Research Group chapters sponsoring consumer legislation; Low Income Planning Aid's initiating or working with local Health Care Coalitions to organize around "Hill Burton" and workfare; the Mobilization for Survival's attempts across the country to influence U.S. Senators and Representatives to vote for the McGovern and Mitchell Transfer Amendments.

Some **strengths** of this type of organizing include:

- usually a high degree of consciousness, at least among organizers;

- good research capabilities (which also means the ability to figure out which issues are winnable);
- organizers are usually well-trained;
- good mobilizing capacity because of a single issue focus.

Some **weaknesses** of this form of organizing include:

- the organizers may run the organization, with the common citizen feeling like a participant in the action, not a determiner of the action;
- if the organization is state or regionally based, smaller cities or towns don't usually share in the action as much as larger cities and towns do;
- possible funding problems may arise.

Community Control Approach:

This approach assumes that if economic education and production institutions are decentralized at a local, neighborhood level, communities can manage those institutions, and that self-management can give the citizen power. This approach sees neighborhoods as the ideal participation mechanism for citizens; it advocates neighborhood self-sufficiency and control of all aspects of the neighborhood, including its economy (community-controlled banks, co-ops, and neighborhood taxation), food production and prices (roof top and hydroponic gardening, food co-ops, community gardens), housing (housing co-ops, rent-control), business and production (neighborhood businesses, small-scale and cottage industries), education (community schools), energy (wood and solar co-ops, shared resources, hydro-electric plants and publicly owned utilities).

There are a number of **strengths** to this relatively new approach to organizing:

• at least ideally, this approach could make the large corporation and the large government bureaucracy irrelevant; it would bring decision-making back to a local, small-scale population;
• it increases the meaning and significance of citizen participation and community organization from organizing against negative consequences to organizing for positive changes;
• it offers many creative possibilities (currently people are raising trout in their basements in Washington, D.C., and are developing solar collectors on top of housing blocks in New York City) and taps human resources/potential/ingenuity currently "laying fallow;"
• it develops community (especially needed in a technological, mobile society);
• it allows people to be in touch with and be responsible for changes and decisions and encourages citizens to educate themselves to issues and hold elected officials accountable.
• it empowers citizens.

Some of the **weaknesses** of this approach include:

• the inability of most communities to make it happen; community control means a reorganization of people's current ways of doing things and a lot of inertia is involved in getting people to change habits (witness Carter's energy plan). Also, the present system doesn't encourage such changes (if you take time to get involved in a community co-op you have to sacrifice much free-time, family time, etc.).

• the tremendous amounts of capital, technical expertise and time community-based organizing requires; researchers are extremely scarce in low-income neighborhoods. The tendency for the "experts" (be they from business, higher education or social service) to take over or influence decision-making is a strong tendency, as the history of most community development corporations will show.

• co-optation: because big monies are often required, government and big business interests will probably be involved; community development corporations especially may find it difficult to be a part of a community organization that demonstrates or confronts;

• changes in goals: if the community group must cater to big business for investment capital it should be aware that that corporation may feel differently about what the community needs than what the community itself believes it needs;

• institutionalization: as the organization continues to work on its organization and development, it may lose touch with community needs, and become irrelevant to the community;

• time: community development takes time to show results;

• growing pains: non-hierarchical self-government is a difficult process to achieve, frought with power-struggles within the community, differences in assumptions and beliefs, and tendencies to establish old forms in new battles.

"Mass-Based" Organizing:

The "Mass-Based" approach is similar to Public Advocacy Organizing in that it usually uses top-down as well as bottom-up methods of defining issues and developing structure. The difference between these two is that "Mass-based" organizing continually seeks and mobilizes its membership (developing a mass base) to work on local issues. Mass. Fair Share's local organizing efforts around local property tax dodgers and slumlords are at least as significant as its state-wide campaign around insurance legislation.

This model of organizing is often a combination of Alinsky and Public Advocacy organizing, and has grown out of Welfare Rights organizing. Some of the National Welfare Rights Organization's leading organizers in the late 60s and 70s have gone on to set up state organizations in California, Massachusetts, Arkansas and several other states. It is not unusual for these state organizations to have annual conventions to take stands on major state issues.

Some of the **strengths** of this approach include:

- usually works on an interesting mix of state and local issues;
- usually well-trained staff;
- plenty of experience in organizing.

Some of the **weaknesses** of this approach include:

- a concentration on one style of organizing, usually confrontational;
- a reluctance to develop local coalitions with other groups because of the concentration on mobilizing its own group and developing its own identity.

Consciousness-Raising Approach:

Consciousness-raising organizing builds issues and develops commitment around a conscious awareness of the problems and their root causes. In small groups, people discuss their current situation and their possible future by exploring how they are oppressed and what they can do about that oppression. The organizer is supposedly well-practiced in group facilitation and knows how to listen well. Paulo Freire, one of the major developers of this approach, sees the organizer or facilitator taking people from *conforming* to society to wanting to *reform* society, to developing methods of transforming society.

The women's movement and the black power movement are two of the best-known examples of this approach. In both cases, an increased awareness of one's condition produced an awareness of the potential for change, as well as the capability to bring about that change. Because most of the problems raised in this approach are culturally induced (sexism, racism, etc.) actions that are established are quite often designed to offer an alternative to that culture (through new lifestyle models, newsletters, alternative schools) or provide a direct service for those most directly oppressed (rape crisis center, legal help around discrimination, drug counseling-rehabilitation).

Some of the **strengths** of this form of organizing include:

- deep understanding of the cause of the problem;
- deep commitment to the solution of the problem, or at least one aspect of the problem;
- usually high energy level;
- usually reaches those directly affected.

Some of the **weaknesses** of this form of organizing include:

- the great amount of time it takes to develop consciousness;
- some people's resistance to probing questions which may be too threatening (no matter how supportive the environment may be);
- some actions possibly becoming social service, not organizing;
- different groups using this approach possibly not seeing the inter-relationship of their own oppression with other peoples' oppressions, and the groups' becoming fragmented from each other. (Blacks, workers, women and youth have never effectively united to fight the economic system, for example.)

LoRie LeiNiNGeR

THE ORGANIZER AS PERSON

While this manual concentrates primarily on the development of analytical skills, there is also a need to develop and use interpersonal skills when organizing a group of people. Keep in mind that your personality and your attitudes are as important as your knowledge of what structure to set up and what action to take. More than anything else, organizing is encouraging people to communicate, to work together and to take risks. You, as an organizer, will be looked upon as model communicator, co-worker, and risk-taker (whether you want that or not).

Here are some things you may want to be aware of before you begin organizing:

1. **Find your own style.** If you're not a Saul Alinsky, then don't try to be like him. Know who you are—your strengths and resources as well as how you come across to others best, your weaknesses (how you turn people off). Plan to use your strengths, decrease your weaknesses.

2. **Be aware of how you feel about what you're doing.** Your values and your attitudes are always showing. If you don't like who you're working with or what you're doing, it's going to come across. If you don't think the type of organizing you're involved in will effect change, you'll be broadcasting it no matter how hard you try not to.

3. **Be aware of why you're organizing.** What's in it for you? People are going to want to know, and you'll probably be asking yourself that question a number of times yourself. Why not begin answering that question now?

4. **Follow up on leads and promises.** If you're going to turn people on to an idea, people will need encouragement and support. You are the one that will have to provide it.

Wayne Friedrich

STEPS INVOLVED IN COMMUNITY ORGANIZING

While there is no doubt a variety of answers existing to the questions raised at the beginning of this manual, there seems to be a basic unity among organizing theorists and practitioners as to the basic steps organizers should take in developing organizations. What is community organizing? Community organizing is, simply, a way that citizens can set up their own organization to reach their own ideals or solve their own problems. The process is first and foremost a learning process, a process where people unlearn dependency and passivity and learn or relearn creativity, decision-making, and an orientation toward solving problems and reaching ideals.

We are what we experience. Psychologists say that attitudes and beliefs rarely change before actions and experiences change. The role of the organizer, then, is to be careful to create a series of experiences that will develop an awareness in people so that they can personally and collectively take control of their own destiny; they can work together to create visions, identify problems, solve problems and implement those visions.

These "series of experiences" can be translated into the following steps:

Define significant issue 	**STEP 1:** *Organizers help citizens state what citizens feel to be their major visions, problems, and needs.* The issues must be determined by *citizens*, not organizers, for it is the citizens who will take control of the organization. If citizens are asked to deal with someone else's issues it becomes that other person's organization. If the organization is to be significant, it must involve significant numbers of people, and work on significant issues. The more significant an issue, the more it deals with fundamental political and economic issues.
Develop structure through leadership, resources, decision-making	**STEP 2:** *People who define the problems begin building a structure that will combine resources and plan strategies.* The organization must allow its members to utilize their personal potential, participate in decisions, and gather other resources. In order for this to happen, resources must be identified and a structure must be set up that allows resources to be properly employed and utilized. Leadership must be allowed to develop and grow and communication must flow freely throughout the organization. Members should be given significant amounts of work, without being overloaded, and they should choose the type and amount of work the group will undertake.
Take action 	**STEP 3:** *Those who have defined the problems and developed the organization gain power by taking action on a certain target.* The issues must be winnable. People won't stay with an organization or movement that goes from defeat to defeat. People need success to overcome cynicism. It is critical to find whatever win there is in any defeat. Even if negative learning is the result, negative learning can be instructive. To quote a leader of a statewide coalition of citizen groups, the issue must "unite, not fracture." It is an age-old tool of people in power: divide and conquer. The political and economic elite in this country remain in power through division of blacks from whites, blacks and whites from hispanics, young from old, tenants from homeowners, etc. Picking an issue, then, should revolve around one which enables several groups to work together and realize the commonality of their situation.
Evaluate	**STEP 4:** *Members evaluate what they've done.* What worked, what didn't and why. Alternative actions.
Define next issue or action	**STEP 5:** *Members discuss and plan future actions or issues.* Many groups lose their membership once the initial battle appears to be won. Band-aid programs and conciliations are intended to mollify citizens and are based on the hope that throwing a small bone to the people will quiet their bark. This is one of the most crucial steps in the whole process; to insure continued accountability and monitoring.

CHAPTER II: IDENTIFYING ISSUES

Wayne Friedrich

Something exciting happens when people decide that they want to act on an issue that is important to them. Take the case of Rick, a 15-year old co-founder of a youth organizing project:

"It all started when some of us kids got bored with just hanging around town. There wasn't anything for a kid in our town to do if you didn't want to get into basketball leagues or eagle scouts. So we used to hang around the center of town just to show people how bored we were. We'd drink a little, smoke a little, get kinda rowdy. And then one day some of us got busted, and suddenly the whole town thought it had a drug problem. Hell, they had a neglect problem.

"Anyhow, pretty soon this older guy started coming around and we figured he was a narc. He'd ask us what was happening, and of course nothing was, then he'd ask us how we felt about nothing happening. We didn't tell him much. I mean, you never know what they're gonna do once you tell them something. He kept talking with us though and asking questions and pretty soon he got us talking about what we could do if we got our act together.

"He helped us start thinking that we were a pretty talented bunch --I mean, we had musicians, artists, cooks, carpenters, people who thought they were pretty good business people. So some of us got to thinking about giving it a try. We figured what the hell-- what'd we have to lose? So we started to put pressure on the city to let us use the basement of an old school building for a coffee house and crafts building and a place to hang around. We got signatures on petitions, met with selectmen and we even got some of our parents to vouch for us. We got a coffee house within four months. And it's still going--for 18 months now--every Friday and Saturday night. Good entertainment, good food; and our craftshop brings in a lot of money for us. Now we're thinking of going back and asking the town for money to keep the thing running all the time. We've learned more from this experience than anything we ever got out of school."

The case of Rick and the coffee house is a good example of what can happen when people begin to get in touch with something that is vitally important to them. Rick decided that something was wrong in his life, and found that his friends, too, experienced something wrong in their lives. When people are allowed to speak what's on their minds, to create visions, to identify problems, they are taking the first step toward building an effective organization.

There are several reasons why this is such an exciting, empowering process:

First of all, it allows people to *identify their frustrations and voice them*, and it allows them to consider seriously their participation in the future. Most people think that they have no right to complain about problems or dream about ideals. We are taught to put lids on our aspirations. Helping people to speak what's on their minds can help people see that they can begin to control the future.

Secondly, it *unifies* people. As people begin to share visions and problems, they begin to see what it is they have in common. Discussion with his friends put Rick in contact with other youths who had the same problem. There develops strength in unity.

Third, it *activates* people. Identifying problems can get some people angry, as Rick was angry. It may get people excited, and motivated enough to take action.

Finally, it provides organizers with the chance to *begin to find and test out potential leaders*. People who are really interested in an issue should be asked what they would do to change that situation. People may volunteer to organize a meeting, to do some research, to call other friends together. Let them.

Achieving this first step is not necessarily simple. **Several processes work against the organizers as they attempt to help people speak out on issues. They include:**

- *The feeling of powerlessness:* People may not want to think about visions or problems. Solutions may not seem evident; problems may be too threatening or the issues might not directly affect them. *Have you listened to the community before you started asking questions? Have you tried less confronting questions?*

- *Irrelevancies:* The issues you choose to ask about might not directly affect them. *Why did you pick this issue? What other issue might be more interesting to people in the community? How do you know?* The key concept here is self interest. What do people really want? A person may have a difficult time relating to the issue of neighborhood when the person really wants a decent apartment.

- *The power structure may see you as a troublemaker* and make it tough for you. If an organizer is doing the job right, no doubt the leaders of the system you are organizing against will see you as threatening. There may be attempts to buy you off, appease you, discredit you, or in one way or another, to threaten you. Be prepared. (**See** "Are We Aware of the Consequences of Confrontation?" and "Have You Planned Alternatives?")

- *People may want to blame themselves for their situations*, instead of understanding how the system makes them victims. And why not? Human service agencies reinforce this attitude, dealing with problems at the individual level (counseling, welfare, special education, etc.), encouraging people to adjust to a sick situation rather than healing the system. The media sets ideals of physical beauty, youth and riches, and offers you ways to change yourself (once in the morning does it) rather than the situation (you wouldn't have bad breath if nutritional standards were changed).

Lionel Delevingne

- *Citizens at least initially will probably resent the organizer.* They may not trust the organizer ("Who is this person? Why is she sticking her nose in our affairs?"), may sense class and value differences ("He speaks better than I do.", "She's too cynical about a system that I've been taught to believe in.").

- *You as an organizer may be tempted to define the issue yourself,* instead of allowing the community to define the issues. This is the major temptation of Step 1: imposing your own agenda. *What are the consequences of doing so in terms of community participation?*

- *Allowing citizens to define issues may lead to some tension between what people believe to be the problem and what actually lies at the root of the problem.* It could present a problem for organizers who want to make sure that organizing can lead to significant social change: *Can organizing around street lights ever lead to the establishment of publicly-owned utilities? Can organizing around human service issues through a mandated agency allow human services to prevent the problems that they are designed to solve? Will your goals put an end to expensive bureaucracy and unresponsiveness, or maybe challenge the relationship between government and the lobbying of special interests?* Organizing around dead end issues, as so many organizers end up doing because they themselves organize without purpose or vision, burns out both organizers and citizens and only temporarily solves problems.

There may be at least two responses to this last problem. One is to determine the issue oneself, and to have people choose the structure, strategy and tactics around that issue. Welfare rights groups and tenants rights groups are two examples. A second approach is to provide a series of questions that help citizens understand power relationships so the groups can effectively deal with the roots of their problems. Consciousness-raising groups and some Alinsky-style groups use this method.

IDENTIFYING ISSUES: VARIOUS APPROACHES

An organizer's first step is to help the community identify a winnable, meaningful issue. While the task is clear, the approaches vary, as discussed in the introduction, because of different assumptions about power, differing amounts of resources, etc.

Alinsky — Style Organizing:

Here an organizer has no agenda but to find out what is needed in a community. The organizer spends a lot of time listening to the community, knocking on doors, hanging around community laundromats, bars and other gathering places, developing trust and doing research. Eventually one issue begins to stand out above all others. Community spokespeople for the issue develop. The spokespeople and the organizer begin to understand and clarify the issue, and find ways to mobilize people around a specific target.

Kayla Kirsch/Jennifer Cobb

Mandated Citizen Participation Organizing:

Most mandated agencies are integral parts of the political economic system. An organizer working for such a mandated agency must first be aware of the possible contradictions involved in being paid by an agency of the system to work for social change of that system. *What kinds of change will this agency allow? Is it enough change? Is it significant?* It becomes important for the organizer to research the agency that pays her, getting a sense of what is possible. The organizer should understand both the *letter* and the *spirit* of the mandate of the citizen group.

Smart organizers use the credibility that the system gives the group to search for leadership and issues. Access to people and information may come easily. Also, since most citizen participation mechanisms are set up to deal with popular issues, your group may have an easy time finding established or credible spokespeople.

Mandated groups, because they deal with other agencies and government officials, and because they deal with a middle-class mentality, tend to attract middle-class participants. Street work and door-knocking and good research can bring in working class and minority people, which can help your agency become more relevant to the needs of most low and moderate income people.

But if you do get community people with gutsy issues, be prepared for a lot of red tape and hassles from your agency, government officials and those you decide are your opponents.

Public Advocacy Organizing:	Community Control Approach:	"Mass-Based" Organizing:
Since the organization has already defined the broad general issue, the purpose here is to help community people see how their specific problems are symptoms or examples of that issue. The problem this approach faces is similar to the one faced by the human services approach—starting out with a "party line" instead of reaching into the community and asking what their concerns are. You may also have a hard time getting people to buy-in to the issue if you don't *relate it* to their immediate needs. Few people want to hear about solar energy when they're worried more about jobs, housing, food, etc. An organizer must make these people see the relationship between, for example, the high cost of utilities and the use of solar power, or the safe jobs solar energy would provide as opposed to the risks involved in nuclear energy jobs. Members of the Massachusetts Franklin County Alternative Energy Coalition seem to have dealt with this concern successfully. When the group took on nuclear power as its issue, it went from town to town and door to door ("We've canvassed the county three times in four years," says organizer Anna Gyorgy, discussing the nuclear power issue). Because it maintained so much contact with people in the community, it has managed to help local people establish energy committees in most every town in Franklin County.	Since the major incentive for using the community development approach is to show citizens that by owning their own institutions they can fight exploitation, the natural first step would be to research where the community is most exploited and what can feasibly be undertaken by the community itself. Lots of discussion with community residents is helpful, but surveys and questionnaires can provide more accurate answers. Remember, those asking the questions will be asking personal questions (Where do you spend most of your money? How much do you spend?) so, unless the purpose and use of the questionnaire is explained well, you may get doors slammed in your face.	This approach adds another dimension to the Alinsky Approach to defining issues. If the sponsoring group has some sort of existing network (regional or state networks, for example), the group's previous research and experience in other cities and towns may help an organizer identify what types of issues appear to be more winnable issues than others. Unfortunately, this information can also be used manipulatively by the organizer or organizing group to establish its own agenda, even though the issue may not be as relevant to the community as it is elsewhere. (The western part of Massachusetts, for example, continually gets lumped in with Boston decision-making though its concerns are very different.)  Courtesy Mass. Fair Share

Consciousness-Raising Approach:

culture, causes and cures

Domestic violence, the battering of women within the confines of the home and an intimate relationship, is one of the most insidious forms of abuse. Using a combination of media, BDIC senior student Sandy Mandel and Joan Kamman of the New England Learning Center for Women in Transition will explore the cultural roots and some of the contemporary reinforcers of this problem. The powerful documentary "Behind Closed Doors" will be shown along with the newly produced NELCWIT video tape to highlight some of the alternatives to abuse at work in the community.

weds, april 12, 3p.m. 615 goodell

This event is free of charge and open to the public

The consciousness-raising approach for identifying problems helps persons identify and understand their own experiences and feelings of inferiority and begin to realize that the source of these problems stems not from themselves, but from oppressive treatment by others in a larger social-political context. Otherwise labeled "personal" problems are seen as political, and their social roots are recognized. Solidarity develops as people recognize a common oppressor. There are two distinct ways people have utilized this approach.

The first, used by such groups as the women's movement and the black power movement, begins with the identification of cultural diseases (sexism, racism) and their causes. Through a series of "consciousness-raising sessions," organizers attempt to help participants recognize and build on their own strengths and develop alternative, constructive responses to these ills. These responses often become collective actions, ranging from rape crisis centers to newsletters to strikes to cooperative economic ventures.

The second approach, developed by Paulo Freire requires the organizer to spend considerable time in a community, getting a good sense of the aspirations of the people in the community, their language and key topics which spark emotion and discussion.

Using the Friere approach, organizers would bring in slides or photos of people, places and activities extremely relevant to the aspirations of the group. For example, to an inner city neighborhood group, organizers might show pictures of poor housing, a landlord's home, city hall, an unemployment line, the most powerful bank in the city, kids playing, teenagers hanging around, etc. As people see the picture, they talk about what they see. "This is how I feel about..." "This is what I think would happen if..." Pictures, then, provide a stimulus for discussing the situations that exist. By asking the right questions, organizers can begin to help people discover reasons for their situation, which is often one of oppression. Further dialog may lead to action. The difficulty with this method is that it requires much time and patience in order to allow the participants enough time to understand their situation.

Our labor of love -- for peace ... for freedom ... for justice

Lorie Leininger

AM I PREPARED TO ORGANIZE?

It's not easy to begin to organize in a community, even if you have lived in it all your life. The first thing that seems to pop up in the organizer's mind is, *Where do I start? What do I look for?* The following question sheet is designed to help you break the ice by helping you understand why you want to organize and who you want to organize, and to identify the power problems you will be dealing with.

The one person you'll be working with all along is yourself. To keep working effectively, you are going to need energy. Your expectations, and the way you come across to others, are going to affect your energy level and your success. If you are unclear about your expectations, or if they continually go unmet, you aren't going to organize for long. Answering these questions can help you better understand the most important person you'll be working with in the community....yourself. The questions are arranged so that you can fill in your answers on the page or duplicate the page and hand it out to your group to fill out individually. It's always interesting and informative to go back and see what you originally thought about these issues when you're many months (years?) along with some cause. It also helps give you perspective and acts as a reminder when you're so embroiled in an issue you can no longer evaluate your progress.

Questions About Myself

- In general, how do I come across to others? To people in the community?

- What are the implications of the image I project?

- How should I dress and talk and listen? Should I work on some specific behavioral and physical changes?
  Comfortably, what is appropriate.

- What does it feel like to be helped? How do I really feel when I can't seem to do something and someone comes along and helps me do it?
  Help makes you feel empowered when someone aids you.

- What does this imply about my entering the community?

- What will I get out of all this? (Why am I in it?)

- Are my motives subject to suspicion from those I want to help?

- Do I feel comfortable handing over power to others?

- What would happen if I didn't get credit for this or I wasn't appreciated?
  Can't take it on yourself if case does not work out as you want.

Questions About Myself and the Community

If I were moderately successful in what I'm doing in this community, what would the community I'm working in look like:

- 20 years from now?

- 10 years from now?

- 5 years from now?

- 1 year from now?

- 6 months from now?

- Next month?

Questions About the Powerful in the Community

If a community is going to change, more than likely it is going to have to deal with those who currently run the community. Political theorists believe that major business and industry are key leaders in the community. Elected officials also play major roles in decision-making. Less important in terms of decision-making, but more important in terms of possible support for you, is the role that social service, civic and religious leaders and clubs play in the community.

You may want to have a number of people fill this out individually (if you're organizing with several other people) and then compare/discuss perceptions about the sources of influence in the community.

— *Kennedy Fellowship*

Economic Decision-Makers: Who are they, and how do they make decisions?

- What major issues have they been involved in recently? How do they affect the community you will work in? — *waterfront involvement. downtown sector*
  — *Dionne Home.*

- What interests are the majority of these people trying to protect?

  Their own.

	Who? (Leaders)	How Do They Decide?	(What boards/committees do they sit on? What social clubs do they belong to?)
Banks			
Major Industry			
Chamber of Commerce			
Who's Who			
Major Property Owners			

Courtesy Valley Advocate

Political Decision-Makers:

- Who are the *U.S. Senators and Representatives* in the area?

- Who are the *State Senators and Representatives* in the area? Moe Montha M.P.

- What form does the *city or town government* operate under? (selectman, city council, strong mayor, etc.)?

- Who are the *chief officials*? STAN LAWLOR MIKE HARRIS

- What major issues have they been involved in?

- How do these issues affect the community you will work in?

- Who are the members of the *school committee?* Betty M.W. etc

- What major issues have they been involved in recently? Merger of St Joes + Scotland

- How do they affect the community you will work in?

Religious, Civic and Social Service Leaders:

- Who are the major *religious leaders?* Pope, Bishop Carter

- Why are they considered leaders?

- Who are the major *social service leaders?*

- Why are they considered leaders?

- What interests are the majority of these people trying to protect?

- Whose support do I need? How will they respond?

Courtesy UMass Photo Center

- What sort of public education needs to be done? What are best formats (newspaper articles and columns, leaflets, radio/TV PSAs, slide-tapes, speaking at schools, luncheons, libraries, etc.?)

- List the sort of research you feel will be necessary and the sort of information you will need about the following community resources:

    Community service agencies?

    Legal services?

    Health planning councils?

    United Way?

HAVE I SPENT TIME IN THE COMMUNITY?

If you want to gain the respect and trust of the community, you're going to have to learn to listen. There are hundreds of ways organizers can do so. Review the possible approaches listed here and pick one or more that best suits your needs. If for some reason you've determined part of the issue yourself already, then use these approaches to think of ways that the community relates specifically to your topic. Remember four things: (1) *be yourself;* (2) you'll need an *issue that a significant number of people can relate to;* (3) those you talk with *could later become part of your organization;* (4) you need to understand some of the *history* of the community.

In general, you should be looking for the following:

People

- people who are interested in changing the community
- people who have problems with the community
- people who will mobilize others in the community (by knocking on doors, making phone calls, etc.)
- political/social leaders and spokespeople in the community
- youth leaders
- elderly leaders
- leaders of groups and organizations
- people who can speak in front of large crowds

Events

- what kinds of events the community supports
- how various sub-groups feel about these events
- which events get the community excited

History

- what successes and failures the community has had in the past 10 years
- level of community activity (high, medium, low) in the past 1-2 years
- key issues, events and people over past 10 years
- economic history

Landmarks

- places that are most often used in the community (churches, businesses, community centers, agencies, etc.)
- places where different segments of the population congregate

INFORMATION GATHERING TECHNIQUES

Here is a list of methods which have been useful for defining several groups I've worked with over the past 11 years:

Sarah Deering

Knocking on Doors

This is just what it says: spending time visiting people in a block or neighborhood, talking, *listening*, asking people about their major concerns.

At first, door knocking felt awkward and seemed to take up an incredible amount of time. But as I got through the 'getting to know you stage,' I began to see that the energy and time was really an investment in the future. As trust built up, people not only went into detail about their concerns, but many began to commit themselves to do something about those concerns as we began to set up a neighborhood organization. People who had never attended our first community meeting in January went en-masse to City Hall in April, picketed City Hall in July, and held the first successful rent strike in Western Massachusetts history in September and October...
—Organizing of the Spanish American Union, Springfield, Massachusetts, 1968

Needs Survey

This is a documented assessment of problems encountered by a specific group of people in a specific area, and can be done almost anywhere people congregate. A needs survey is like a poll; it usually takes the form of a prepared questionnaire. Going door-to-door, hanging out at the laundromats, street corners and bars, or getting the survey printed in the local newspaper or aired on radio or TV (especially cable or public TV) are all worth exploring.

We felt that we'd have to know the major concerns of the community before we could do anything else. Five or six of us listed categories that we felt we and others in the community experienced. We listed them on mimeo paper given to us by a local church. We left plenty of room for people to write their own suggestions. We got a local youth group to help us go door-to-door, to shopping centers and churches, wherever people came together. Our visibility helped people know we were concerned, and that people were anxious to see results. Some who were interviewed interviewed others and the project really snowballed. Our data not only gave the organization something to work on, it also helped us get government funding...
—Organizing a Neighborhood Council, 1975

Public Hearings

The success of a public hearing often depends on who is putting it all together, and for what purpose. Here's what one author says of some traditional public hearings held by city officials and organizations:

> *Some time is spent on trivial formalities, announcements, and occasional testimonials. Meanwhile, nervous claimants frown and fidget as 'their' time passes. The officials proceed to set the stage. Some are seeking to enhance their recognition as benefactors, others to put the claimant on the defensive. By the time the preliminaries are out of the way, the claimants are understandably prepared for a bloody confrontation. The procedure often produces hostility.*
>
> —from "The Future of Citizen Involvement," in The Futurist, December, 1975.

Public hearings often sift out certain segments of the population—those who are inarticulate, feel uncomfortable in large gatherings or are intimidated by authority, don't feel comfortable enough to speak out or don't believe they'll be heard. As a result, many concerns aren't represented. However, there are other cases—when citizens hold their own public hearings—that yield different results:

> *We spent a lot of time getting media coverage and enlisting specific people to attend the meeting and have their say. We made sure that those who gave testimony asked questions that got to the root of the problems, yet were asked in such a way as to put people at ease. People applauded statements that others made. People enjoyed themselves, and the media loved it.*
>
> —Organizing the Children's Campaign, 1974

Community Research Manual

In this case, small groups of people act as a nucleus of a project that involves many others in a community statement of problems and concerns.

> *Our council's first of five state mandates was to determine the major children's needs in a geographic area that included six cities and towns. We decided to really take that first mandate seriously, assuming that if people really owned the need or problem, they'd really be motivated to do something about it. So we surveyed the schools in the area, as well as adults. Kids who had been surveyed, surveyed their parents. They had been through the process and enjoyed it, so they wanted to take others through the process. Human service specialists in several areas gave us their research, or helped us write the manual. Because people knew that they were stating their concerns and their resources and knowledge, the manual became theirs. In short, several hundred people helped in various ways to research, type, print, distribute and act on the manual.*
>
> —Organizing the "Children's Yellow Pages," Holyoke-Chicopee Area Council for Children, 1976

DEVELOPING TRUST

One of the early hurdles organizers must get over is that of developing the trust of people in the community—especially if organizers are new to the neighborhood. As organizers raise issues and expect people to risk themselves to work on issues, members of the community may become quite suspicious of the organization, and unwilling to participate in any of its activities.

As you are going about the business of doing outreach, try asking yourself these questions:

Yes	No	
X	___	Am I open to people (and to myself) about why I am organizing? Am I clear about the purposes of my organizing?
X	___	Am I clear to people about what my methods will be?
___	X	Are the issues that I raise too threatening? How can I make them less threatening?
X	___	Am I clear about what I want people to do? Do I give them various options for participation?
X	___	Do I show that the participation can make a difference? What's in it for them? Is their time worth it?
___	X	Is my dress or appearance threatening?
___	X	Is my manner threatening?
?	___	Am I in touch with my feelings as I talk with people? Can I communicate feelings in a way that can benefit communication?
X	___	Do I know the history of organizing in this area?

IDENTIFYING THE ISSUES: MAPPING A STRATEGY

Possible Data Gathering Places	Names of Places/ People	Questions to Ask in Each Situation	What I Need to Know From the Answers	Ranked Order of Importance
Door-to-Door	(Locations, districts)			
Gathering Places				
Places Where People Experience the Problem				
Where Problem is Treated				
Places to Get Literature on or Documentation of the Problem				
Where to Get Information on Root Causes				
Supporters of Target Group				
People Who Cause the Problem				

Because of time constraints, organizers need to map out and prioritize the best places to identify the problems. The adjacent chart is a planning grid to help you do so.

Column 1 asks you to state the various places where the kind of data you need could be best gathered: door-to-door; gathering places (laundromats, bars, playgrounds, etc.); places where people experience the problems (if consumers are angry about the high prices at a local market, talk to them outside the market); places where the problem is treated (human service agencies, hospitals, health clinics, counseling centers.

Column 2 asks you to think of the kind of data that interviews with persons in each of the areas can provide.

Column 3 asks you to generate the kinds of questions that need to be asked of each source in order to get the data you need.

Because an organizer's time is precious, *Column 4* asks you to prioritize the places to be contacted.

GATHERING INFORMATION EXERCISES

1. The Community Interview

Minimum no. people: 2
Minimum time: ½ hour

It may be helpful to your group to have those who will be doing the organizing brush up on interviewing skills. This can be done by using the role-play situation below. It can be done by breaking the group into pairs, with each person then filling out an evaluation sheet after the interview, or by having a pair go through an interview process with others observing and filling out the evaluation sheets.

Setting: Use the context you will be organizing in. For example, if you will be organizing students in a high school, role-play that situation. Set the scene by stating what the organization is all about, and why they are asking questions of people. Have one person play the role of the organizer, and others play community people with the following roles (assign these roles by handing out role-descriptions on sheets of paper so no one else knows who the others are supposed to be):

- a person who at first feels the organizer has no right to ask those questions
- a person who is strongly against the position the organizer is taking
- a person who cannot stay on the subject
- a person who continually says, "Don't ask me...what do you think?"
- a person who incorrectly defines the solution to the problem
- etc.; whatever fits your situation.

EXERCISE: The Community Interview

INTERVIEW FEEDBACK SHEET

This feedback sheet is designed to help the person who has just interviewed you learn what he or she did that was helpful, and what he or she did that could be improved. Spend approximately five minutes filling out this sheet, then hand the sheet to the interviewer and explain feedback and comments. Criticism should not be shied away from, but should be done constructively.

```
poor        great
 1 2 3 4 5           1. The interviewer made a good initial impression.
                        • My attention was captured
                        • I wanted to continue the conversation
                        • My initial impression of the interviewer was


 1 2 3 4 5           2. The interviewer listened and communicated well.
                        • Discussion was allowed
                        • I felt I was heard
                        • I felt I was understood
                        • I could understand what the interviewer was saying


 1 2 3 4 5           3. I felt support and help.
                        • I was helped in developing my ideas
                        • I felt I got beyond where I was before I started the conversation
                        • I was given other resources that could help me
                        • I was given the most help when


 1 2 3 4 5           4. A trusting relationship was developed.
                        • I did not feel threatened
                        • I did not feel inhibited
                        • Specific behavior that built or blocked trust was when


 1 2 3 4 5           5. The interviewer left on a positive note.
                        • I felt like I'd want to talk to this person again
                        • The impression I was left with at the end of the interview was that it was


 1 2 3 4 5           6. Other criteria


 1 2 3 4 5           7. Other criteria
```

EXERCISE: The Resource Interview

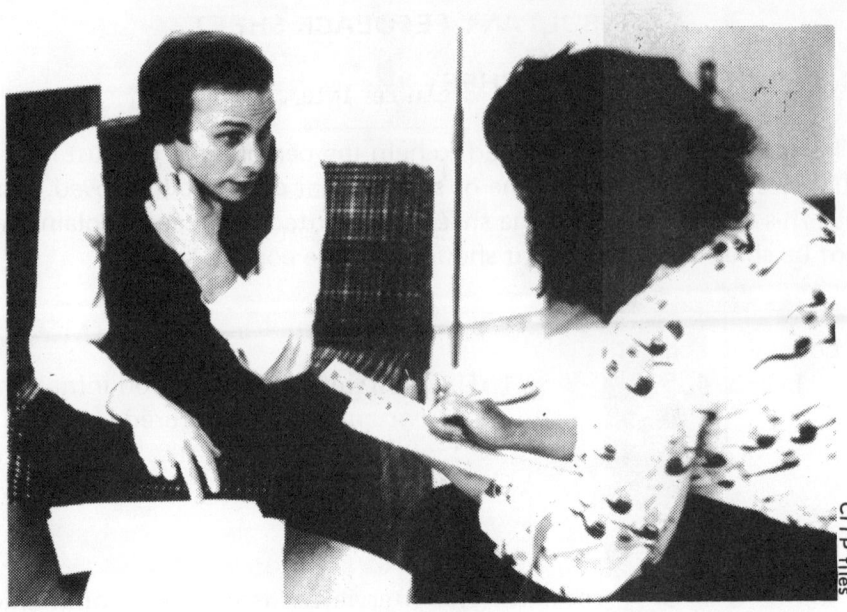

2. The Resource Interview

Minimum no. people needed: 5-10 organizers or community people; 5-10 outside people
Minimum time: 1-1½ hours for interview
for evaluation

This exercise can be used to help practice interviewing skills with community officials and can begin to get the kind of information you will need as you start to work on issues. This session requires the use of people outside your group (consultants). These people will be interviewed by the people from your own group who want to be trained in interviewing techniques. Organizers should be prepared to ask these people a number of questions concerning the information the group needs concerning specific relevant issues.

Those who are facilitating the exercise will need to contact resource people who are knowledgeable about the problems to act as interviewees. They may be social service people, politicians, as well as other people working with these problems in the community. They may represent several viewpoints.

Process:

1. Seat the consultants around the room (spaced far apart) with an empty chair facing each person being interviewed. Organizers will then begin interviewing by moving into the empty chairs, introducing themselves and asking questions. They should keep the interviews brief and move to the next chair when it becomes vacated. Organizers should be instructed in advance that they are interviewing for two purposes. One purpose is to get information. The other is to conduct an effective interview which will be evaluated at the end of the exercise by the consultants.

2. The consultants or agency people should write the name of each trainee who interviews them on separate Consultant Feedback Sheets and briefly fill out that form after the organizer leaves and before the next one comes.

3. At the end of the exercise (allow about 1-1½ hours), collect the evaluation feedback sheets from the consultants and put them aside. Ask the consultants to join a general evaluation session with organizers, where together organizers and consultants can give their impressions.

4. After the discussion is over and consultants have left, you can give the organizers their personal evaluation sheets. Ask them if there is anything about them that they would like to discuss.

CONSULTANT FEEDBACK SHEET

Evaluation of Organizer Interview

Name of Organizer _____

1. Did the organizer present him /herself well?

    Yes   No   O.K.

2. Did you understand the purpose of the interview (the information she/he wanted)?

3. Did you withhold any information because of something which was said or done?

    If yes, what information?

    For what reason?

4. What was the general mood of the interview in your opinion?

    ☐ hostile   ☐ friendly   ☐ indifferent
    ☐ boring   ☐ interesting   ☐ pleasant

5. What things would you tell the organizer to do differently next time?

    1.

    2.

    3.

6. What were some of the positive things about the way the organizer conducted the interview?

    1.

    2.

    3.

3. Participant Observation

Minimum no. people: 2
Minimum time: to be compiled over several weeks

Participant observation* is a process of combining research with action to solve problems. It is based on the assumption that research and action on problems can be done by people most affected by the problems—local community residents.

A participant observer is an investigator gathering evidence. Like Columbo or Woodward and Bernstein, the person amasses data about a particular problem by watching, searching for clues, following leads, interviewing key informants and making interpretations from the evidence to reconstruct events. The participant observer is concerned with facts; impressions are not useful unless verified by investigation. Observations are carefully recorded; judgments flow from the evidence. Observations and reports are pieced together carefully and woven into a persuasive case.

Participant observation helps answer questions like: *How are things happening? What things are happening that we usually don't ask about? Under what conditions are they happening? Why are they happening?*

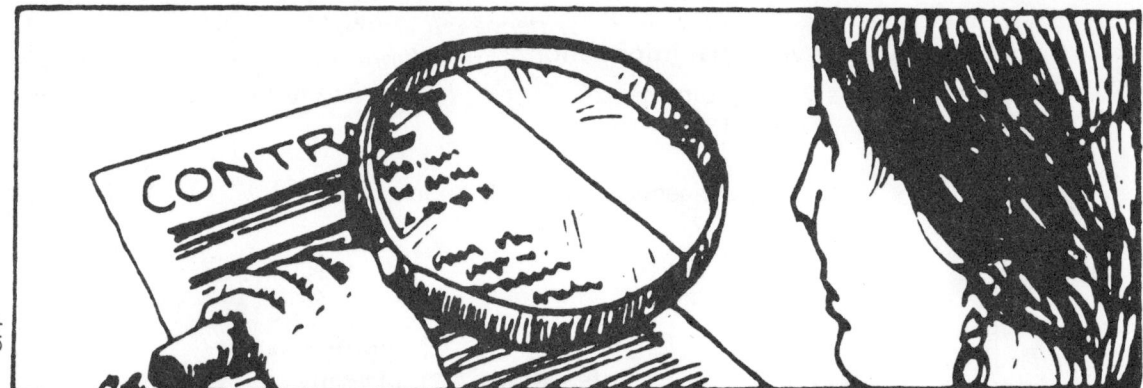

Process:

1. Mini-Observations—each observer makes a 15-minute visit to any location (e.g., laundromat, restaurant) and immediately afterwards records all data observed. Following that, the group comes together and each person reports on what was seen. (You might wish to do this in small groups.)

This exercise will enable you to become more aware of the wide variety of things that are "observable." *What is significant about the setting, the costumes, the overall situations?*

2. Conversations—attempt to memorize the key parts of a conversation. Don't try to take on more than a half-hour or so the first time. Record the data immediately afterwards. Piece it together. *What does it say?*

This exercise is a good way to learn to "tune in" to a conversation. You will find that you can remember more than you thought you could.

3. Memory Tests—try to "tune in" on 10-minute segments of other people's conversations. For instance, try to listen carefully to 10 minutes of a school committee or City Council meeting. *Who said what to whom and in what sequence?* Once again, record the data immediately after leaving the situation.

4. Community Observations—visit a community scene in a team of three or four. Observe the street scenes and the actors. *What are the major institutions? What are the people like? Is there much interaction? What socio-economic characteristics stand out?* Once you've done the observation, meet as a team and put together a "community analysis" based on the one observation. Present it to the other teams and vice versa. The exercise will promote your ability to observe community influences.

---

*from **Collecting Evidence: A Layman's Guide to Participant Observation**, by Joseph Ferreira and Bill Burgese.

5. The Neighborhood—ask the principal of a neighborhood school to arrange for a group of three or four of you to visit the school in your neighborhood. Ask to tour the building, sit in on the classes, go to the cafeteria and talk to a few teachers. At the end of the day, sit down as a group and list the things that made an impression on you; develop another list of areas for further inquiry. Call back and ask the principal to let you look into those situations for further inquiry. This is more than an exercise, it is the beginning of a citizen study of the school.

6. Trace Effects and Wear Spots—if you buy a Coke from a vendor and notice when you throw the flip-top away that the rubbish barrel is full, you might think that the vendor is doing a brisk business. A display window pane with nose and finger smudges is likely to indicate that little people are stopping at the window to look. These are trace effects. The dirty or worn rug in front of a display case in a store is a wear spot. For an entire week, note the traces and wear spots you see, as you go through your daily routine. List them each night when you get home. This will sensitize you to be aware of this valuable, often overlooked form of evidence.

7. Group Study—attend three or four meetings of the same group, making participant observation notes immediately after each. After the sequence of meetings, list each "piece of evidence" on a separate card and then put them together. *What story does the evidence tell you? What is the group about? How do they see themselves? Is their real business the same as their "stated" purpose? Can you sum up the meetings in one or two sentences?* Discuss your findings with a friend. If you plan to observe groups, this is an important training exercise, well worth the effort.

Wayne Friedrich

WAYS TO PRIORITIZE PROBLEMS

No doubt when you are working in a community you will come upon a number of people who have a number of different types of problems. It is important that the community work on a few problems at a time. Here are some ways to help the community decide which problems it should deal with first.

1 Voting:	2. Group Discussion:	3. Team Building:
Here the entire group brainstorms problems or issues, which are written on a blackboard or piece of newsprint. (During a brainstorm, allow any ideas no matter how far-fetched. Do not censor them.) Once ideas are up, have everyone vote for their top three (four, five, six or whatever) issues. Those receiving the most number of votes are the top priorities.	For more discussion and reflection on certain issues, after the brainstorm, break into small groups around specific interest areas that were brought up during the brainstorm, and have these small gruops further clarify and restate their small group concerns in terms of proposals. After plenty of discussion time, have the small groups submit their proposals to the large group, and have the entire group vote on those proposals as in Number 1. **Voting.**	For more emphasis on team building, after brainstorming, the large group would break into pairs. Each pair selects and agrees on two priorities. This should take about five minutes. Next, pairs join together to form groups of four persons. Each quad selects two priorities from the four possible priorities that the pairs brought with them. This should take about eight minutes. Next, the quads then join to form groups of eight and again reach consensus on the two top priorities. Allow 12 minutes for this process. Finally, the process continues until the whole group has merged and agreed upon common priorities, or it could be combined with another decision format, such as described in Numbers 1 and 2 (**Voting, Group Discussion**).

Wayne Friedrich

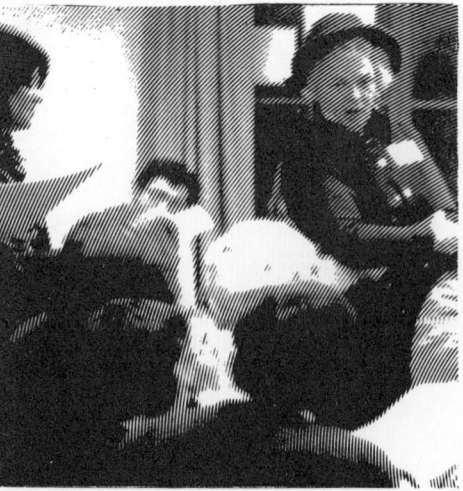

HAVE WE DECIDED ON AN ISSUE?

Now that you have canvassed the community and have done some community research, you should begin to think of ways to bring people together to try to do something about the issue. Listed below are some of the ways that organizers do this. Perhaps this will help you formulate a strategy that would be best for you.

There are some things to keep in mind:

- *make sure you give some thought to how the group chooses and talks about an issue;*
- *you don't want to divide the community into factions—rather, you want to mobilize people in the community; Which issue appears to do this?*
- *you want to build community leadership and ownership in the issue as soon as possible;*
- *if you have momentum in the community, you want to keep momentum going;*
- *at the same time, you don't want to raise expectations unnecessarily; you may or may not want media coverage;*
- *you may or may not want certain people to attend;*
- *be very clear about the purpose of the meeting: let the purpose determine the agenda;*
- *people are more apt to testify and to give information at a public hearing if they feel that something positive will be done about that information;*
- *be prepared to follow through;*
- *hold the meeting at a time and place convenient to those who have the problems.*

Ways of Bringing the Community Together

1. You can call together everyone who has discussed a specific problem with you, and at a meeting propose specific strategies to deal with the problem, or devise a meeting format which allows participants to propose strategies.

2. You could have one of the people you interviewed in the community call together those she knows who are also incensed about a problem to discuss the issue and strategies. Or you could call the meeting jointly.

3. If you don't feel you have a significant enough issue and you want to get more public response, you could hold a public hearing, inviting all members of the community to speak out. You may want to give special attention to being sure that people you have had discussions with get their sentiments heard. You may want to help people plan testimony. Keep in mind that many of the people who were so open with you in an interview might feel intimidated in front of a large group—take this into consideration when formatting the hearing.

4. You may want to call a small number of people together to act as an *ad hoc* steering committee to plan a larger community meeting.

How Others See the Problem

What the problem is really depends on who is defining the problem. Different segments of a community tend to see a problem in different ways, which often results in conflict. Those who live and work in a community see the problem differently from the power structure of that community; regional and state legislators may see it differently from both groups, and a community organizer may have even another version.

If any of these segments is going to be able to work together to resolve a problem, they had better be aware of how the other group(s) see(s) the problem, and clarify whenever possible. One way to do so is to fill out the matrix on the next page.

46 You may want to add other categories to the matrix—how other social change groups perceive the community; how the community, power structure, government, etc. perceives the organizer, etc.

How the: community	local power structure	general public	social service agencies	government (state, federal)	other
perceives the problem					
perceives the solutions					
perceives the community					

- *Where are the differences?*
- *Why do they exist?*
- *Which differences do you need to clear up first?*
- *What can be done to clear up the differences?*

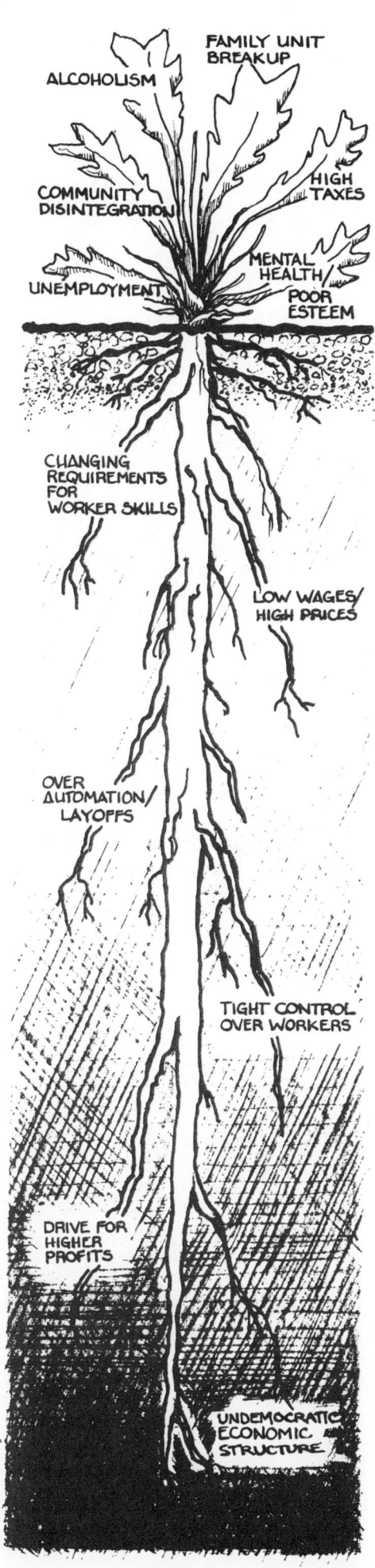

IDENTIFYING ROOT CAUSES

One of the pitfalls that most community organizations fall into is defining a problem which is really a symptom of a larger problem that continues to go unsolved. What usually happens is that the organization may win some small victories around an issue, but it soon finds the same issue or related issues cropping up over and over again.

For example, a group of youths and adults in a small town in Massachusetts became concerned that many teenagers in their community were dropping out of school, beginning to commit crimes, and generally raising Cain in the community. Some of the most serious offenders were involved with drugs. Hearing in the media and from government agencies that drug programs could provide counseling for drug-dependent youths, the group spent 13 months organizing a drug treatment program for the community. Using such slogans as "Youth Power," and drumming up support from many segments of the community, the program succeeded in receiving both local and government funding. It was able to provide counseling and therapy to the 120 or so youths who came to the center each year for help.

During the third annual meeting of the agency, someone who had noticed an increase in school drop-outs and youth crime since the inception of the program stated his concern that the program wasn't doing what it had set out to do; many teenagers who used drugs may have learned how to cope with the problem of drug abuse, but the reasons why teens abused drugs in the first place still existed. The director of the project replied that perhaps 3-5% of the youths in the community came to the drug center and admitted that one of the weaknesses of the program was that it wasn't designed to prevent drug abuse. The problem, as the director saw it, was that the community couldn't really deal with the drug and crime problem until it created jobs and a meaningful place for youth to go in the community.

Like many programs born out of community organizing, the drug programs in this town had responded to the symptoms of a problem—drug use—and did not deal with the root causes of the problem—no role for youth in the community. Under the guise of mobilizing and empowering people, the town had set up a bureaucracy that helped some, but did not prevent the defined problem.

This approach can have even more serious consequences.

In his book, **Blaming the Victim**, William Ryan talks about the tendency of society to blame those who suffer from a problem for that problem. He provides a four-step process by which this happens:

Kayla Kirsch/Jennifer Cobb

Steps	An example
1. Someone identifies a social problem:	Unemployment.
2. A group of "experts" studies those affected by the problem and identifies the ways in which the "victims" are different from the rest of the population as a result of deprivation and injustice:	The unemployed are lazy, ignorant and unskilled.
3. The differences are then defined as the cause of the social problem itself:	They need motivation to work.
4. Usually a government agency is assigned the problem and mandated to invent a humanitarian action program to correct the differences:	Unemployment compensation, CETA, Job Corps, etc.

Because of our tendency to blame the victim, those who may have been mobilized to act on a problem become "serviced" instead.

Organizers often fall into the trap of working on these ill-defined, symptomatic issues, either because their job description says to do so, or because their "constituency" defines the issues that way. Blaming the victim becomes a strong belief in our culture. Organizers, too, end up blaming the victim. Let's face it, blaming the victim is also easier than tackling the real problem.

By looking at the root causes of the problem and acting on the root causes, this tendency can be reversed.

Donn Young, Valley Advocate

HOW TO GET TO THE ROOT OF THE PROBLEM

Here are two different types of responses an organizer could make to an unemployed person who is distressed about situations in the community:

Blaming the Victim

Organizer: *What's the problem?*

Joe: *I can't find a job.*

Organizer: *How do you feel about that?*

Joe: *Rotten. Pretty worthless, I'll tell you.*

Organizer: *How long have you felt this way?*

Joe: *Since I was laid off last year.*

Organizer: *What have you done about it?*

Joe: *Looked in all the newspapers, called the unemployment agency and visited social service agencies, the whole trip.*

Wayne Friedrich

Root Cause Questioning

Organizer: *What's the problem?*

Joe: *I can't find a job.*

Organizer: *Yeah, I guess you're not the only one. Seems to be a lot of people out there who can't find jobs. Got any ideas why?*

Joe: *Guess I just don't have the right skills.*

Organizer: *I don't know about that—you worked for eight years as a draftsperson with Bendit. You must have been pretty good.*

Joe: *Yeah, I guess I was . . . but Bendit moved south last year.*

Organizer: *They aren't the first, are they? A lot of factories seem to be moving—how come?*

Joe: *Guess they can get cheaper labor down there.*

Organizer: *So you're unemployed because the factory owners wanted higher profits, not because you're unskilled.*

Joe: *I guess so. So big deal. What good do those skills do me now?*

Organizer: *They could be put to work helping us set up a worker-owned factory. We're negotiating now with the City Council to . . .*

Root Causes:
A FEW UNDERLYING ASSUMPTIONS

Increasingly, social and political scientists are contending that many people are powerless because of an economic structure that rewards a few at the expense of many. Here are some facts and figures that you may be able to use to educate yourself or others with whom you work. These facts and figures may be disconcerting to some. They are not meant to discourage, but to help all those who are organizing to look realistically at the kind of struggles needed to help people achieve a real sense of power.

Ferdinand Lundberg, in his book **The Rich and the Super Rich**, states that **1.6% of the population owns over 32% of the wealth** in this country.

This 1.6% owns:
- 82% of all stocks and bonds
- 100% of all state and local bonds
- 88.5% of all other bonds
- 29.1% of all cash.

Money is finite. The more some people have, the less others have. This can be graphically understood by looking at how income and wealth are distributed among various populations.

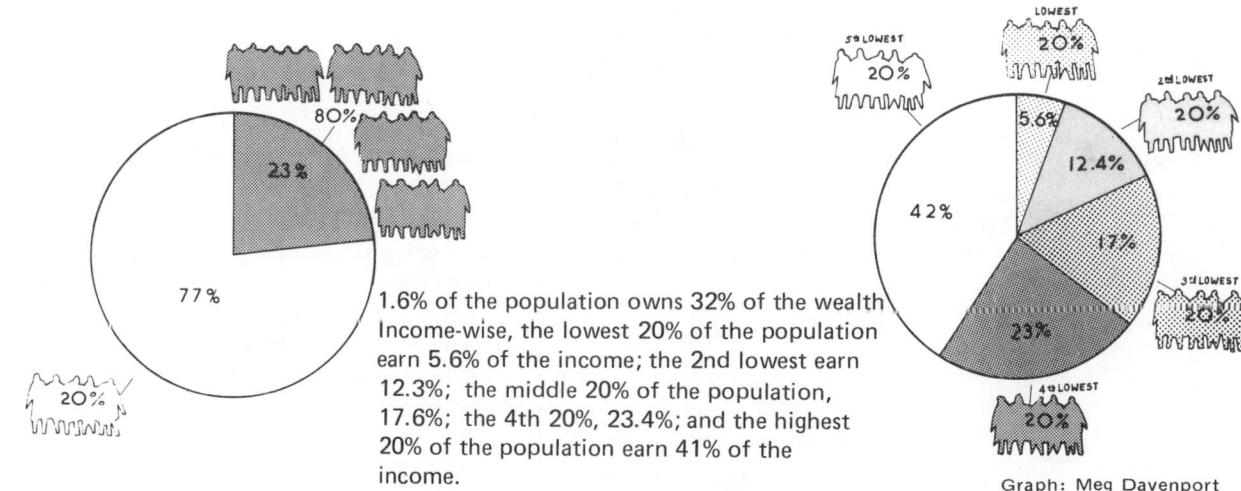

1.6% of the population owns 32% of the wealth. Income-wise, the lowest 20% of the population earn 5.6% of the income; the 2nd lowest earn 12.3%; the middle 20% of the population, 17.6%; the 4th 20%, 23.4%; and the highest 20% of the population earn 41% of the income.

Graph: Meg Davenport

Additionally, almost all the major industries are dominated by a few large corporations. In 1950 there were 440 beer companies in the United States—there are now only 48; the top four (Bud, Schlitz, Miller and Pabst) control two-thirds of all beer sales. In 1961, Phillip Morris sold only 9% of all cigarettes in the United States—today it controls one-fourth of the market and, together with R. J. Reynolds, sells two-thirds of all cigarettes. Phillip Morris, the second biggest cigarette company, *now owns Miller*, the third biggest beer company.* For the United States' 213 major manufacturing industries, the top four companies in each case control an average of 42%—almost half— of the market.

National priorities in terms of fiscal spending are also skewed. At present, 54% of our tax dollars is earmarked for military expenditures; only 22% of our tax dollars is spent on human services.** Human service organizations, then, are mandated to alleviate problems which are deep rooted—on a shoestring budget.

For the United State's 213 major manufacturing industries, the top 4 companies in each case control an average of 42% -- almost half -- of the market. (House Committee on Judiciary, *Investigation*.)

The Workbook/cpf

***Business Week,** March 24, 1973; November 8, 1976; December 6, 1976.
** Figures compiled by the Library of Congress Legislative Reference Service as released by Rep. Les Aspin of Wisconsin.

Greenfield (Mass.) Recorder, Tuesday, May 9, 1978

Greenfield moves to keep Bete

By LARRY RIVAIS
Recorder Staff

Greenfield selectmen Monday decided they will approach the Channing L. Bete Co. with suggestions for keeping the expansion-minded business within town limits.

The decison came following the board's reading of an information package provided by the firm, outlining the company's past growth and its projected needs through 1988.

According to the package, the company seeks 10-15 acres on which to build an 18,000-square-foot office building and a 43,000-square-foot printing and distribution center. The company, which employs 92 full-time persons in the production of "scriptographic booklets," expects to need a total of 87,000 square feet of space within 10 years.

In announcing the move, which the company hopes to make from its 45 Federal St. office by mid-1979, Bete listed 11 site requirements, including available utility services, a "growth trend in the tax base," a favorable "tax rate trend" and low development costs and interest rates.

Selectman James A. Fotopulos said he was glad to see the Bete company find a need for expansion. "This is a positive situation," he said. "This is not a crisis. We can cope with it."

The Bete information package also was sent to Northfield, Bernardston, Montague, Deerfield, Gill, Erving and Whately, as well as to the Massachusetts Department of Commerce and Development and the Franklin County commissioners.

With the newly-created town planner's position unfilled — and possibly to be reconsidered in a town-wide referendum if a petition drive is successful today — the board Monday moved to consolidate the town's economic planning committees and to quickly contact Bete President Channing L. Bete Jr.

Selectmen said they will contact all members of the dormant Greenfield Economic Development and Industrial Corp. (GEDIC) to see if they will take an active role in working with the Bete company. GEDIC last year fought unsuccessfully to keep the Millers Falls Co. from moving out of Greenfield.

GIDAC board member Simon L. Cohn said he spoke with Bete Monday afternoon about the 15-plus acres available on Munson Street. Although describing Bete as "non-committal" on the question, Cohn said he urged Bete to "most seriously consider" moving to that property. "We think it would be tragic if he left Greenfield," Cohn said.

What does this mean for the individual, the citizen and the community?

First of all, this uneven distribution of wealth directly affects consumers, workers, working conditions and the general quality of life because prices, production and products are controlled. It means that a lot of decision-making power accompanies that wealth. Corporations can afford to lobby, influence the public through the media and buy their way out of certain predicaments. The larger the corporation and its resources, the more resistant it is to attack or reform.

Corporate decisions affect us in the community as well. Corporations can control working conditions and job availability (automation, speed-ups). Factories use local resources and pollute land, air and water. Towns can become economically dependent on factories, and a runaway factory (one which moves to the south) in turn affects the kinds of educational and health facilities towns can or cannot attract. This in turn affects future influx of people into the community (people may be hesitant to move to a town with poor educational facilities), which in turn affects local businesses, rent

FRANKLIN CO. SHORTS
GARY NIELSON

Another Millers Falls Tool?

The letter came as a complete surprise. Last week the Channing L. Bete Co. of Greenfield sent word to state, county and local officials that it needed a new place to live, momentarily ushering in dark memories of this time last year, when Millers Falls Tool was threatening to run away to the profit haven of Dixie. But, for the county this time, the prospects didn't seem so bad. For Greenfield itself, however, how bad the situation is remains to be seen.

The Bete company, employer of 92 workers on a $1 million payroll, informed the state Department of Commerce and Development, the chamber of commerce, the county commissioners, Western Mass. Electric Co. and boards of selectmen in eight county towns that it has "reached a point where we must consider a major relocation of our entire operation" by next year—and would like to have a new site tightened up by October. Bete, a publishing company, says it needs more elbow room; the number of employees and its sales growth rate are expected to double by 1983, the company claims.

Fortunately, the land of cotton isn't on the company's mind. Company President Joe Bete told the *Advocate* that "we want to stay in Franklin County." He has indicated firmly that he will consider a move only within a 15-mile radius of Greenfield, keeping his firm inside the county. Any proposals submitted from outside "will be shelved." For now.

Bete's announcement had a touch of the dramatic; it was like a spring offensive with that effective element of surprise. No one, but no one, said they had any idea Bete had growing pains.

They know now, and everyone, but everyone, will undoubtedly try to lure the company, its payroll and its property taxes, to his or her town. No sooner had Northfield officials opened their mail than selectmen vowed to go all out to seduce the business, bragging that they are "a better town" than any other on Bete's list—a fat list that also includes Bernardston, Greenfield, Montague, South Deerfield, Erving, Gill and Whately.

Teasing each other during their May 9 session, county Commissioners Jack Bassett of Montague and Meg Herlihy of Deerfield joked that Bete would look really good in their respective industrial parks. **Don Saint Pierre**, the county's economic development specialist, admits that Deerfield is best prepared, with its industrial park already welcoming its first tenant, the Millers Falls Tool Co.

President Bete has said he wants a new site with "aesthetic appeal as well as functional appeal." Deerfield might meet those qualifications and, according to Saint Pierre other, "not so sexy" sites do exist in other towns.

But what about Greenfield, a town that has just lost one of its biggest employers and soon may have to reckon with a super mall in Hadley? The commissioners, Saint Pierre and his boss, **Fred Muehl**, agreed last week that "keeping Bete in our regional center" is a number one priority. Saint Pierre wants to avoid "creating suburban pockets" in outlying towns, particularly with an industry Greenfield already has. "Greenfield first," cheered Muehl.

The bottom line, says Saint Pierre, is that, if Bete leaves Greenfield for anywhere else, it could be "the straw that broke the camel's back, a catastrophe."

"Catastrophe?" asks Greenfield selectman **Frank Yetter**. "That's a pretty strong word. Any firm that leaves Greenfield is not in Greenfield's best interest, but I have every expectation that Greenfield will be successful" at keeping the firm in town. Yetter says that the selectmen have scheduled a couple of meetings with Bete to "assess his needs and desires."

Speaking of meetings, Bete also will be meeting with commissioners, Saint Pierre and planning board members from the towns which he has fingered for possible relocation sometime early this week.

And, while Northfield grabs for the spotlight, while Greenfield struggles to keep a growing industry in town, while Saint Pierre chants possible "catastrophe," the situation could be worse. "If there are no compatible sites in this county," Bete told us reluctantly, "we would, of course, have to take a whole new look."

Don Saint Pierre, Franklin County's economic development specialist, says that if Bete leaves Greenfield it could be "the straw that broke the camel's back." (Diane Young photo)

Valley Advocate, May 22, 1978

LNS/cpf

rates, taxes, town planning and local decision-making.

If a town loses its factory, and unemployment increases, the local realtor or banker who owns two-thirds of the downtown area may suddenly become very powerful because townspeople need that person's financial support. If he wants to build a shopping center over the town common or if he wants to zone farmland commercially (at the expense of local farm survival and local food production), so be it. He also then has indirect control over editorial policy in local media (he is, after all, a big advertiser) and the future of many small businesses.

Corporate wealth has also affected us personally, through the values and messages communicated through television, magazine and radio commercials. Needs are created for many commercial products by exploiting our insecurities and desires for acceptance and status. Competition is accentuated. It is a difficult influence to escape.

Drawing by S. Gross; Copyright 1973
The New Yorker Magazine, Inc.

ROOT CAUSE QUESTIONS TO ASK OF YOURSELF AND YOUR GROUP

Here are some questions you might be able to ask people you are working with to help your group deal with root causes:

1. Is the program you are working for a solution or a response? If a response, how adequate/inadequate is it?

2. Will that kind of solution really solve the problem, or put band-aids on immediate, visible symptoms?

3. Who really benefits from the problem?

4. Who really causes the problem?

5. What would an ideal situation look like?

6. Why do people usually work on symptoms and not root causes?

7. What kinds of resources exist which could help deal with the root causes of the problems at hand?

8. How can you make sure that your organization won't alienate people from each other: black from white, women from men, employed from unemployed, etc.?

9. Does your group have adequate representation of minorities on its board (if applicable)? on its staff? in decision-making?

10. Does the statement of goals and objectives reflect root causes of the problem?

11. Can you join with other groups that are or could be working on root causes? Can you join with labor unions?

Some organizers and human service workers have begun discussion groups in their organizations around these sorts of questions. Discussions revolve around how they can educate themselves and others to be more responsive to the needs of those they are working with. Books such as **Blaming the Victim, Creating the Future and Regulating the Poor** (Piven and Cloward) are often used as discussion pieces.

Lionel Delevingne

Lionel Delevingne

CHAPTER III:
HOW STRUCTURE DEVELOPS POWER

Once you have a bunch of energized people ready to get going, you'd better make sure that there is a process for channeling those energies. That process, or structure, deals with goal-setting, decision-making, leadership, and resources. Like everything else, some structures work well, others do not. Here's an example of one that has proven not only effective and efficient but has also significantly affected the future of grass-roots citizen efforts.

THE CLAMSHELL ALLIANCE

The Clamshell Alliance was born in July, 1976, as an attempt to stop the building of dangerous and wasteful nuclear power plants in New England and specifically to stop a proposed plant, in Seabrook, New Hampshire from being built. Meeting for the first time four days after the announcement of the approval of the plant (and just a few days before the bulldozers moved in), the "Clam" was not only under extreme time constraints, but also it was battling the major pet project of corporate leaders—one-third of all industrial investments had been put into utilities, and the focus of utilities had become nuclear power.

"Our strategy," commented an early organizer of the Clam, "could only be massive non-violence. Court litigation and all other channels had been exhausted."

How successful could the Clam be? Within 300 days after its birth, it had managed to occupy the site three times: the third time by over 2,000 well-trained, committed people. The 1,414 who were arrested that third time on May 1, 1977, were so committed and so well organized that, "We agreed to stay in jail in order to prove our point," according to one occupier. Successful because of a well thought out structure, this group brought the issue of nuclear power home to millions of Americans through the media, forced the reactionary Governor of New Hampshire to appeal for financial contributions (he got none), and provided the major contribution to what many feel to be the most important protest movement of the 70s: organized resistance.

The secret to the structure of the Clam is essentially a trust in the power of the people. Their method was to decentralize— to allow people within the organization to make the organizational decisions which affected their lives. One of the early founders of the group recalls that during the initial meetings, *"We wanted to prove that the organization would truly gain strength by showing trust in the people. We established a set of principles that put that into the structure."*

Their decisions were as follows: (1) there would be no leaders. A Coordinating Committee was set up to *coordinate* decisions made by several local groups, not to *make* them; (2) the Clam methods would be non-violent direct actions; (3) the first focus would be on Seabrook; (4) each local group would maintain its own existence; (5) the group most directly affected had "blackball" rights on any action because the local group best understands the political climate. Only that group could say "no" to an Alliance project. If other groups didn't agree, they didn't have to participate.

"Again, we wanted everyone to be heard, and felt that this structure was the best way to do it. There were some who were asking, 'doesn't consensus decision-making take a lot of time?' and my response was, 'yes, at first it does because we aren't used to it; but once we got skilled at it, it worked a lot more quickly.'"

As the group began to plan its major occupation, in May of 1977, its structure became even more participatory, through the establishment of "affinity groups." Anyone who would occupy the site would have to join such a group; thus by April of 1977 there were literally hundreds of these affinity groups.

Lionel Delevingne

Affinity groups became the vehicle not only of decision-making, but of training. Affinity groups were composed of 10-15 people who had gone through non-violence training together (non-violence training was a prerequisite of the occupation). Each affinity group elected a spokesperson (called "spoke"), who often rotated the job with others. Spokes were responsible for bringing decisions, ideas and proposals from the affinity groups to a larger body of spokes. Spokes only conveyed information back and forth; affinity groups made the decisions. This made for **decision-making from the bottom-up** instead of the traditional handing-down of reforms and decisions from government and bureaucracies.

Each affinity group also had a medic (who received training and some supplies), a media spokesperson and several people designated to deal non-violently with agitators. Affinity groups served not only as decision-making bodies but also as small community units or neighborhoods and enabled occupiers to police themselves, monitor the area for outsiders (anyone who didn't have an affinity group that could identify them was asked to leave), and keep track of/look out for each other.

"What the training did was to put power into our own hands. First, it allayed our fears. Each of us in our affinity groups discussed previous run-ins we had had with violence. We had a chance to discuss what we were doing, and why we were doing it. We weren't going into this blindly: we clarified our feelings. We went through mock role-play experiences to learn how to make decisions collectively under pressure and how to deal with outside agitators. We also role-played the occupation itself. Those who role-played police later shared with us how it felt to have to arrest us and carry those who resisted. It helped us see the police as people—fellow citizens—who probably didn't like the situation any more than we did. We were continually reminded that the police are not our enemy—nuclear power is. That was a significant change from the 60s; the 'pig' mentality only served to isolate sides. I think our training helped us gain the cooperation and sympathy of the police and I'm pretty sure it helped avoid confrontation..."

The advantages and personal results of the structure are best related by one of the participants:

"There's a whole list of things that I got out of the Clamshell structure. First of all, I got a sense of security. I knew that no decision would be made unless I was consulted. That's important to know when you're about to be arrested for a non-violent act. Secondly, it built a sense of community. My affinity group became my ad hoc family, and we made deep friendships going through the many crises together. Also, I felt ownership—or maybe partnership—in the occupation. I felt responsible for how well it went. The training that the structure had set aside ahead of time prepared us as groups capable of making decisions. This put power in everybody's hands. We had to think through consequences beforehand.

"Our process flabbergasted the other side. They had the opposite style of decision-making: the National Guard would have to call headquarters (and probably the Governor) before they

The occupation was so well structured it even provided an *Occupiers' Handbook* which gave legal information, listed what to pack and outlined several hard-and-fast rules all occupiers had to agree to, such as no alcohol or drugs, no running, no fires after dark, etc.

The occupation itself has been deemed a major political success. Over 2,000 people occupied the site and 1,414 were arrested. Knowing full well the consequences, the 1,414 spent what amounted to over a week in jail. Because of the affinity group structure, the persons were able to win concessions from the less organized, hierarchically-structured National Guard. And since then the 1,414 and others have been busy educating and organizing future actions.

Lionel Delevingne

could make a move. Our ability to make decisions on-the-spot, (including decisions to hold sit-down strikes, hunger strikes, and so on) won us privileges. Because we could out-maneuver them, we were able to secure exercise periods, natural foods, vegetarian meals, showers, a library and phone calls. Our decisions were made literally out in the open. Everything was open and honest.

"Not least of all the experience turned around my previous feelings of impotency. It showed me that we can have power, and make a difference. It was different from my experience of the 60s. We had alternatives here, we had an organized battle plan, and it was more than a march to a monument. It was fought like a war."

Chad Dobson, an organizer of the Boston Clam, remarked while discussing the internal workings of the Clam, "Everyone agrees that our internal workings allow us to have the community that's necessary to fight something as large as nuclear power. The internal is every bit as important as the external."

Another Clam organizer said, "It was consensus decision-making that did it. If a group can't reach consensus, it may not be time to act. My advice to other groups is, when the time is right, when people are ready, then move. We got 2,000 ready, then we moved."

DISCUSSION: THE ROLE OF STRUCTURE IN ORGANIZING FOR POWER AND CONTROL

Structure can contribute immensely to the success of the community organization, or it can work toward its downfall.

Using the Clam as a case study, it is possible to understand some of the dynamics of structure.

1. The Means Dictates the Ends: That is, the structure educates us as to how to act.

If we experience a structure that is hierarchical, we think and act hierarchically (or we spend a lot of precious time trying to forget that hierarchy). Underlings wait for leadership to give direction and orders, and may become involved in leadership struggles. Leaders assume "correct postures," because they are on top and need to show they're in control. Feelings are replaced by the structure's "logic." *Top-down* decision-making puts participation, ownership, and control in the hands of those few on top, and makes the rest of the organization dependent on the leadership (and at times resentful of that dependency). The consequence is that decision-making can be done quickly, but may have questionnable support and more likely alienation and dissatisfaction of the membership.

It's also important to remember that change begins at home. Many organizations looking to change the system employ identical structures with the system it is trying to change, when it is usually the structure that is at the root of the problem.

Alternative newspapers are a good example of this. Most are run like traditional newspapers—hierarchical management. Yet articles and editorials promoting worker-control, and equal rights and decrying other evils of the system abound. Your structure should model the type of world you're trying to work toward. If you can't do it at home, how can you pull it off on a community or global scale?

Decentralized, consensus decision-making structures, on the other hand, can allow participation and ownership by everyone. People are needed for the group to operate, and tend to want to share ideas, help decide the direction of the organization, and participate in the action. It allows everyone to be useful and taps the creative potential of all. It doesn't make people feel like pawns.

The Clam set up a structure that allowed people to make decisions for themselves. The structure not only succeeded during the occupation, it continued throughout the jail process, much to the consternation of the National Guard.

2. The Structure Determines Which Resources—Internal and External—Get Used and How: Internally, good use of membership resources can determine the direction of the organization and commitment of members to the organization and the issues. A good internal structure provides everyone with the ability to participate meaningfully, and utilizes the individual's participation to the fullest. The more a person participates, the more both the person and the organization benefit.

Too often, groups require little participation from anyone but the leadership. The resources and capabilities of most members go unknown and untested.

Good use of external resources further determines the capabilities of the organization. Community organizations have always relied on churches, social service agencies, labor unions, sympathetic politicians, and other grass-roots or social change organizations such as theirs for support. These kinds of support mechanisms exist in most every city and town.

Lionel Delevingne

3. The Structure Influences Leadership and Leadership Influences Structure: Flexibility can work wonders here. Initially, the group should be allowed to experiment with different leaders. Many fledgling groups set up steering committees, locate chairpeople, and use these chairpeople more as facilitators than leaders.

This serves several functions. (1) It keeps the group committed to the purpose rather than committed to a leader. (2) It allows people who haven't had a lot of experience with group process to get some practice, so that when crisis decision-making is needed, they are skilled and prepared and the group doesn't fall apart.

A common disease groups catch is that they lose that flexibility as the group matures. *Different types of leaders will be needed at different stages of any organization's growth.* If the organization is seen as a living entity needing different kinds of nurturing, and not as the child of one single leader, it will be easier to find ways to share, support and rotate leadership.

4. Decision-Making Power is the Key to Commitment: Despite what Madison Avenue would have us believe, people want to determine the direction of their own lives. If they see participating in community action as an important part of their lives, they want to have jurisdiction over what the group is going to do, and how it is going to do it. Community organization is an active process.

Once a leader or an organizer makes decisions for other people in the group, the sense of community is lost. You can't expect people to be passively active. People should be allowed to get together to determine goals and objectives of the organization.

Lionel Delevingne

The Clam's decision-making process not only brought about commitment to the specific task at hand (the occupation), but it brought about a commitment to deal with the larger issue of stopping nuclear power.

"Some of us thought that an occupation of 180 people (the second occupation) could close the plant. We now see it as a long, continuous struggle, with no quick solution,"

says Dobson. When asked what this did for morale, he replied:

"We saw that our judgment was off, but our commitment was there. We were hooked on participation. The courts feel that by socking us with stiff penalties, we'll be persuaded not to occupy in June of 1978. This just isn't true. What really is happening is that people won't be put off by it. Just yesterday two people dropped their appeals and are going back to jail. The Governor of New Hampshire has made a mistake. People are taking on a renewed spirit: some are even planning their vacations around sentencing dates."

Once upon a time, there was a bunch of people who were stuck in a hole.

FOR THE ORGANIZERS:
TYPICAL HASSLES IN DEVELOPING STRUCTURE

attempts were made by various individuals to get out of the hole...

such as desperate arm flapping...
...meditation and levitation...

...jumping...
This went on for hundreds of years, until they had tried everything except helping each other out...

so they helped each other out.

Courtesy Tenants Handbook
New Brunswich Tenants Committee

This is testing and maintenance time for the organizers. You'll be dealing with a lot of process—"how" kinds of questions. *How are we going to make decisions and govern ourselves? How are we going to participate? How will we involve other groups?* Although this period is not (usually) the noisy, media-involving time other periods in the history of the organization are, it is nonetheless essential, for it lays the foundation for success or failure. For the organizer, it is a period of working behind the scenes—helping a group choose goals and objectives, allowing leadership to develop and practice, observing a group as it makes decisions and giving feedback, helping a group develop its membership and its external resources, and measuring the ways that a group takes responsibility for itself. One of the organizers for the Boston Clam sees his role as such:

"There are many ideologies in the group. Some see the Clam as part of a non-violent movement. Others see it as a Marxist-Leninist organization. We're not just interested in getting more people; we deal with other maintenance issues to keep the vitality that allows us to be able to work together. My main goal, my most serious responsibility, is to keep everyone's mind on the goal, and help them understand ways of maintaining their commitment to a viewpoint while still struggling towards that goal. It takes lots of interpretation, lots of reminding of the past, and lots of politicking within the organization."

Here are some problems that you as an organizer may face during this stage of development:

1. People may not want to take responsibility and leadership: This is probably a new experience for them. Many people (women, hispanics, etc.) have been negatively reinforced for this in the past and are coping with societal constraints that have led to a lack of confidence.

- What kinds of ways can participation be less threatening, and yet allow people to become committed to the group? How can people be encouraged to participate and speak out without communicating condescension, tokenism or prejudicial reactions to their ideas and abilities?
- What are people's motivations for joining the group?
- What are the visions and expectations of the group?
- What kind of leadership does that entail?

2. A few people may take on too much responsibility and will not share leadership. (See same questions as above.)

- How can you point out the way their behavior affects others (in a non-threatening manner)?
- How can you get others to take control of the situation?

3. People may not be clear about goals and objectives.

- What are the shared visions of the group?
- What are the differences? Can these differences co-exist or be overlooked in order to work together? Will the differences divide? How can they be dealt with?
- What is the problem the group is trying to deal with?
- What are the options?
- Are they realistic?
- Which are winnable?
- Which is top priority?

Sarah Deering

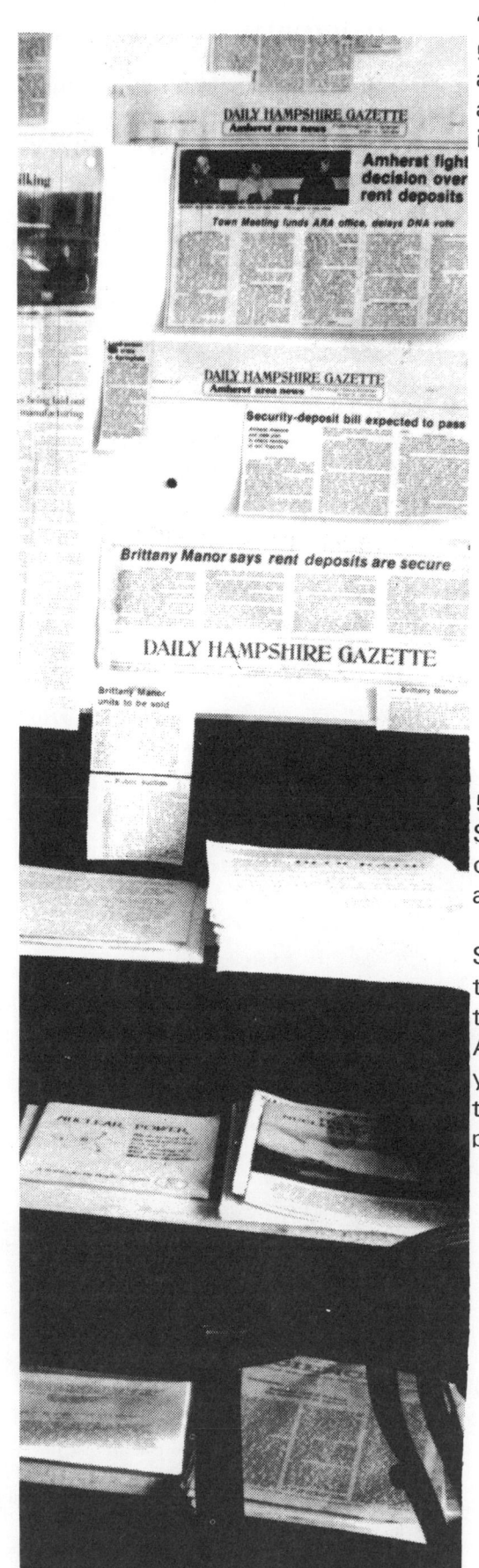

4. We don't seem to have enough membership. The Clamshell's homogeneity (mostly middle class whites) is considered as both a strength and a weakness by many of its members, although local Clam groups are beginning to do more grassroots organizing in working-class and in low-income communities.

- Why do you feel the group needs more membership?

- Who do you want to join you?

- What motivation can you provide these people to get them to join?

- How have you used members in the past? (Pick several members that have stayed on and several members that have quit and analyze reasons for staying on/quitting.)

- Is there anything about your group that discourages new membership (clannishness, power in hands of few, too many failures, too much work...)?

- How are people who are not members of your group affected by the problems you are trying to deal with? How might they participate?

5. I want to take leadership. Ah ha! This is the temptation of Step No. 2, and many group leaders—and their groups—have gone down because the founding fathers and mothers have become precious about their baby.

Sometimes the organizer is on a power trip, or is too impatient with the process of building leadership and takes control. Other times the structure creates a situation which sets the organizer up as leader. A mandated council, for example, may elect new members every year or even every two years, but the organizer may stay on for three, four or five years, becoming the most visible, reliable spokesperson for the group, and therefore the natural leader.

- How can you find people in the community to do what you're doing?

- How can you convey/transfer the skills you have to others?

- How can you help others develop ideas?

- Think harder—what other options do you have?

- How can you build on the strength of the group to make it want to take responsibility for itself?

- How can you build into the structure a mechanism which encourages members to keep control out of the hands of a few?

APPROACHES TO DEVELOPING STRUCTURE

Alinsky—Style Organizing	Mandated Citizen Participation Organizing:
Much experimenting and testing goes on during this period, as people who may never have been a part of a community organization practice running an organization while at the same time becoming concerned about an issue. Positions, roles, goals and objectives should be clarified before action is agreed upon. Especially in times of confusion, community members should be aware of a tendency of staff to manipulate. People will be participating for various reasons, and will exhibit various levels of involvement. More established members should take care to insure that new members feel a part of the organization (that they have a meaningful function) but do not burn themselves out of the organization.	There seems to be a tension in this approach between "what we're supposed to do" and "what we want to do." This often develops into a form of schizophrenia, both for members and for organizers. I think that the only way to deal with this schizophrenia is to recognize it and deal with it by agreeing who you are, and how you want to relate to the larger organization. Most mandated councils have a structure that has been pre-established by bureaucrats. The design of the structure was set up primarily to meet the needs of the bureaucracy, which may or may not meet the citizens' needs. *How much decision-making are you allowed? What style of decision-making is allowed? To what extent can you use a non-hierarchical approach? What kinds of resources (budgets?!) are made available to you? What kinds of leadership styles? Who will these leaders communicate with in the bureaucracy?*  Tom Knight, Valley Advocate

Public Advocacy Organizing:	Consciousness-Raising Approach:	Community Control Approach:
Organizers here spend time and energy helping community members take increasing levels of responsibility for the organization by encouraging participation in actions taken by the organization and by establishing citizen boards of directors, citizen committees and advisory boards.	Consciousness-raising groups go through several structural stages. The first is the "awareness" stage. Here the structure is informal, and organizers act as "facilitators" to help people become aware of issues and concerns. Sensitive ability to relate to people on a "feeling" level, a deep understanding of the causes and symptoms of oppression, and some awareness of group process are skills necessary for facilitation of such a group. As the group moves into action, it must be allowed to start whichever structure it needs to achieve its goals. Because most consciousness-raising groups recognize that hierarchy is at the root of their present oppression, they tend to work on a collective decision-making level.	Here the decision-making structure is egalitarian, but problems arise. Technical experts are often brought in to provide resources for decision-making at this point, but often end up totally confusing local residents by their technical language. Related to this, since resources are scarce or sometimes expensive, community groups may tend to go with the first technical resources available, even though those resources don't deal with the most important needs of the community.
"Mass-Based Organizing:" Supported by the resources of the larger organization, local mass-based organizers set up local Alinsky-style groups, making significant attempts to develop grass-roots leadership. The organization is usually able to provide leadership training, newsletters, and in some cases regional and state conventions to determine priorities and take stands on state-wide issues. Decision-making in the organization is usually both top-down and bottom-up, and staff manipulation is always a temptation.	 Our Bodies Ourselves/CPF	 CPF

STRUCTURE CHECKLIST
HAVE WE UTILIZED RESOURCES WELL?

EXERCISE: Resource Assessment

Here are some questions that can help you better determine and use your resources. Spend 20 minutes in pairs or in small groups sharing these questions among yourselves, taking notes on newsprint; then share the answers in a larger group and deal with the issues that come up.

1. How do people get recognized in the organization?

2. How can people best feel secure in the organization?

3. How can people in the organization best use their own resources?

4. What internal resources (from the group) do we need to get where we want to go?

5. What external resources do we need to get where we want to go?

6. What external resources exist? Who might possibly support us? (Make a list as large as possible—get others to brainstorm with you. Then see **Target Segmentation** for ways to make the list helpful.)

7. Are there success models elsewhere that we can call on as resources?

8. (If part of a network of organizations): can our network or affiliation with other organizations act as a resource? How?

9. What is the role of the organizer in this process? Will that role help the organizer work herself out of a job?

Minimum no. people: all members of the organization
Minimum time: 30 minutes

It is important to the continuance of any organization that each member of the organization be looked upon as a participating, resourceful, interested member. In order for this to happen, members can be polled or interviewed in order to determine individual expectations and resources. This can either be done informally, as people get to know each other, or more formally through a questionnaire. If it is done informally (some people do not react well to questionnaires) then it should be compiled by the organizer and referred to often to insure the organization is actively using each member. If you think people will fill out the questionnaire, have each member of the organization fill one out. Encourage members to be specific; encourage people to brag. When the sheets have been completed, allow the group to see each other's sheets, to see what kinds of resources exist. Try cataloging skills, interests, expereinces and expectations on a single sheet of paper to have as quick reference. Handing out a copy of the cataloged resources along with addresses and phone numbers can lead members to call on each other more frequently.

Name: _____

Address: _____

Phone: _____

1. I see the goals of the organization as being:

2. I joined the organization so that the following would happen (be realistically idealistic):

3. In order for this to happen, I need the group to:

4. I will probably lose interest in the group if:

5. I have the following skills that I could share with the group:

6. I have the following interests that I would like to explore with the group:

7. I have access to the following people who would be helpful to this group:

8. I have had the following experiences that I feel would be beneficial to the group:

EXERCISE: Utilizing Member Resources

EXERCISE: Utilizing Community Resources

Introduction

Those who are affected by a particular problem can be referred to as a *target group*. Too often, the target group is stereotyped, and its members and institutions are approached with bias. Yet, the fact is that the target group contains persons at different levels of helpfulness to the organizing group. Some members of the group might be more easy to reach *(available)*, more important *(powerful)*, or more *responsive* to the issues. Because the organizing group has limited time and resources, target segmentation, choosing those segments of the target population that will most easily and quickly benefit from your investment of time, becomes a helpful tool to the community organizers.

Steps

The following is a simple process for identifying segments of the target group which relies on easy-to-get information. It requires you to (1) identify the various attitudes people have toward the issue, from most positive to most negative; (2) list all the groups and individuals who fall into these categories; (3) assess the availability, powerfulness, responsiveness, and affectedness of each of these groups and individuals; and (4) prioritize the list.

Here is a step-by-step example of how the process might be done, using the example of a youth environmental group.

Identify attitudes

Step I: Set up a continuum of behaviors and attitudes toward your issue, from the strongly supportive to the strongly opposed. For example:

	strongly endorse	leaning toward support	uncertain	leaning toward opposition	strongly oppose
STEP I Attitudes and Behaviors	Financial support Volunteer to help Write letters of support	Show interest in ecology and the environment	Apathetic	People who feel that kids are too irresponsible People who feel they have other priorities	Speak out against
STEP II Individuals and Groups	Conservation Commission Rod and Gun Club Science Classes Scouts Audubon Society	School teachers Radio station Families who are given information about conservation trails	Newspaper Selectmen	Town Planner	Developers Certain fiscal conservatives Certain realtors

Step II: List all those who are in any way involved, either for or against, according to where they stand in the continuum. Looking at the continuum should also give you a sense of how much work you have to do to win your issue.

List those involved

Step III: Determine which targets are most important to go after. Here are some criteria to use. You may come up with other criteria from your own experience.

- *availability:* the degree to which you have methods to reach the people involved. Put A's next to those you have easy access to (3 A's = extremely accessible, 2 A's = accessible, 1 A = fairly accessible, 0 = not accessible).

Assess resources

- *powerfulness:* the degree to which the person or organization is large, powerful or meaningful enough to make a change. Working with a few college students who are looked upon by the public as hippie radicals might not be enough to sway public support. Pursuading a labor union or county commissioner to support you may be a more substantial change agent. Put three, two, one, or zero B's to indicate the amount of influence and power of these groups.

- *responsiveness:* the degree to which the target group is likely to be responsive to your efforts to effect change. Put C's next to those groups or individuals you feel are most/least responsive to discussion.

- *affectedness:* the degree to which certain groups will be affected by the change. Use D's to designate degree of affectedness.

Step IV: Now take all the "actors and actresses" with letters after their name and place them in a prioritized list by adding the numbers of letters together to rank order the groups. The list should give you a pretty good indication of which are the most worth the time your group has to spend. Then, figure out strategies to use with each group.

Prioritize

The following is an example of how teenagers who were trying to set up nature trails across the state of Massachusetts used Target Segmentation to determine which resources to work with.

Accessible	Powerful	Affected	Responsive	Total	Rank
Human Service Professions					
Scientists					
Environmental Groups					
"Favorable" Legislators					
Ministers Association					
Unions					
Media					

RISK-TAKING AND WORKING FOR CHANGE

The likelihood of involving people in an organizing project can be established with reference to the risks and rewards that participation entails for them. In the case of social change, rewards come in the form of seeing problems solved, or knowing one is contributing to a worthwhile project.

Risk includes economic risks (perhaps even loss of of jobs), spending valuable time, the threatening of one's self image or friendships. The basic strategy for the organizer is to understand and lower the risks for the members and to be aware of and increase the rewards. Risk-taking can be growth-producing if handled well. Below are listed some general traditional risks members take in joining an organizing project, and some general methods of reducing risks.

Risks:	Tools to decrease risks:
1. Takes a lot of personal time	• plan to cut out unnecessary meetings • prepare person for commitment • show that commitment will make a substantial difference • find others to take on some of the responsibilities • plan time well
2. Acting without sufficient information	• get the person adequate information as soon as possible • empower person to get information herself • be specific about the kinds of information that is needed
3. Fear of losing	• plan winnable victories • convince people that the struggle is worth the loss • get "credible people" to participate in the struggle • ask "what's the worst thing that could happen to you" and deal with that response
4. Possibility of losing job or money	• plan winnable strategies • develop a "we'll help each other out" approach • emphasize the effect of current problems on job and happiness • do not ask people to do anything they'll regret or aren't committed to • show understanding and support if people feel need to back down

Now try filling in your own situation's risks and rewards:

RISKS OF JOINING THE ORGANIZATION	HOW TO REDUCE THE RISKS	REWARDS

Minimum no. people: representative number of new and old members
Minimum time: 20 min. questionnaire; 30 min. discussion

Here are some questions that can help you improve the leadership of the organization. Spend 20 minutes in pairs or in small groups asking each other these questions, then share the answers in a large group and deal with the issues that arise.

1. *What kinds of responsibilities does the leadership have to deal with? How is this being done now? Is it satisfactory?*

   What would be the best leadership structure?

   What do members have to learn? How can they learn it?

   Who are some potential leaders?

2. *How should leadership be selected?*

   What do you gain from this selection process?

   What do you lose from this process?

   What are the strengths and weaknesses of other processes?

3. *What is the role of the organizer in this process? How will it help the organizer work him/herself out of a job?*

EXERCISE: Leadership Assessment

SEVEN WAYS TO BUILD COMMUNITY LEADERSHIP

Mark Lindberg has written an interesting booklet, *Up The Ranks: How Community Organizers Develop Leadership*, for the New England Center for Community Organizers (NETCCO). Lindberg lists several principles in developing leadership. The first is that leadership is developed through experience, mainly the experience of action. He then gives seven ways to go about doing it.

Since those seven ways appear to be valuable information for community organizers, they are listed below, with possible methods for achieving the intended results.

After reading them you might want to spend a half hour in small groups discussing how these seven methods might be implemented.

1. **Give potential leaders a job:** actually, everyone in the group should have some job or responsibility, but a leader/coordinator may need special kinds of jobs, such as: researching information, holding meetings at her home, calling other people about meetings or group events, facilitating the meeting, generating ways to solve the problem.

2. **Create obligations for potential leaders:** "Can you speak at the Council of Churches meeting about this issue?" "Can you be the spokesperson at the news conference?" "Can you attend the conference on housing in Boston?"

3. **When possible, let peers convince potential leaders to act.** *Is there someone, or are there some people, who feel strongly about a possible leader, and can they talk with that person about taking leadership? Who are some of the natural community leaders? What is the network of leadership?*

4. **Pick a leader who is directly affected by the issue.** *Who's being ripped off most by the problem? Who has an extremely creative ideal? Who has an extremely practical ideal?*

5. **When necessary, manipulate the situation.** Organizers, because they usually have more time to devote to the issue than most community members, may see shortcuts in bringing issues to

Lionel Delevingne

a head. Doing so may develop one or more new leaders.

6. **Heighten emotions to bring people into action.** The Spanish-American Union in Springfield, Massachusetts, had people write down their housing problems and talk about how a citizen court which dealt only with housing cases would help improve their situation. Other groups try to personalize and freeze the enemy.

Some ways to do this include: having members share with each other how they experienced a particular problem—how they felt, what they did, what they learned, etc.; have people bring in physical evidence of a problem (dead rats can really shake up a landlord-tenant meeting); try some guerrilla theatre (having members act out the problem in a melodrama); calculate or compile facts and figures (people working on the Transfer Amendment in Western Massachusetts figured out that their Congressional District would get $25 million in federal monies if the amendment were passed and used this as a rallying message).

7. **Graduate leaders to new levels of experience:** Maybe it is time to have members of the group meet directly with some of the power figures involved in the issue. Or perhaps your group might become involved in new areas. Why not give some of your responsibilities to potential leaders so that you can work on other levels also?

GROUP DECISION-MAKING: MEANS TO AN END

Minimum no. persons: representative number of members
Minimum time: 20 minutes for questions; 30 minutes discussion

Here are some questions designed to help you think about your decision-making process and to help you clarify what needs to improve. Spend 20 minutes in pairs or in small groups sharing your answers to these questions, then share the answers in a larger group and deal with the issues that arise.

EXERCISE: Decision-Making Assessment

1. Who decided the goals/objectives of the group?

   How were they decided?

2. How are most major decisions arrived at?

   Are you happy with this process?

   Do you feel represented in the decision-making? If not, how could this be improved?

3. How are most crisis decisions arrived at?

   How are most operational decisions arrived at?

4. *How do you know when you've made a decision?*

   How do you record decisions? How do you know everyone understands the exact decision reached?

   Does voting alienate you? Does consensus alienate you?

   Are all opinions heard? Is there a mechanism for incorporating dissenting opinions into the final decision?

   Is enough time spent on decision-making? Too much time?

5. *What stands in the way of the "ideal" decision-making process?*

   Is there a way around it?

   What decision-making process is best to accomplish what you have to do (without sacrificing steps for efficiency)?

   (If mandated group): Will your ideal decision-making process conflict with the decision-making process that has been established for the group?

Graphically mapping out the communication patterns involved in your decision-making process can help you understand your current process and what you would like it to look like in the future. Spend about 15 minutes filling this out alone, then share in small or large groups.

Here are some common communication patterns:

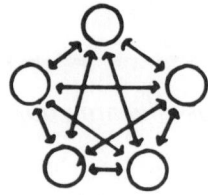

Central Director   **Consensus or vote**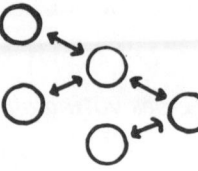

Hierarchical

Now draw the communication pattern evident in recent decisions your group has made. Draw one for each of (at least) four decisions—if they are not the same, your process is not consistent.

Now draw an ideal communication pattern for your organization.

What are the things you would have to do to make this pattern become a reality?

**A WAY
TO IMPROVE
THE DECISION-MAKING
PROCESS**

Movement for a New Society is a national organization committed to social change. The group has written a book, **Resource Manual for a Living Revolution**, which discusses ways to improve the decision-making process of change-oriented organizations. Here is what they have to say:

1. Recognize when the decision-making process breaks down and review task functions ("What are we doing?") and maintenance functions ("How are we doing it?") to see which ones are not being performed. Continue the meeting, having people fill the missing roles.

2. Design a model that brings about more democracy.

3. Have the group set the agenda.

4. Rotate the facilitator and process roles.

5. Periodically, check with the group to see how people fell about the issue, the meeting, and the group process.

*Actually, group process and decision-making are subjects which can only be touched on in a unit on organizing. If you feel that your group is having serious problems with these areas, refer to the CITP unit on group process and organizational development by Bob Biagi.

CHAPTER IV:
TAKING ACTION

CASE HISTORY #1: The Alternative Energy Coalition

New Age Journal

"...Lovejoy choreographed a case with one eye on acquittal and the other on community consciousness..."

TALE OF TWO TRIALS

By HARVEY WASSERMAN

"...At 2:00 A.M. on the freezing-cold morning of George Washington's Birthday, 1974, a weather tower crashed to the snow in Montague, Massachusetts..."

The tower belonged to the Northeast Utilities Company and was the precursor of a nuclear power plant. Its function was to test wind direction, as required by federal atomic siting regulations. It had been 500 feet high, but when the morning sun came up, only 149 were left standing.

The tower's fall was not accidental — it was engineered by Sam Lovejoy, a twenty-seven-year-old organic farmer. He did it by using a crowbar to unfasten three of the tower's twenty-one supporting guy-wires. And as soon as he finished, he ran to the nearest road, flagged down the first car — which happened to be a police cruiser — and got a ride to the local hoosegow, where he asked to talk to the chief.

Shall We Be Moved?

Aside from destroying $49,000 worth of utility, what Sam Lovejoy had just done was introduce the use of open civil disobedience into the American environmental movement.

What he had also done was put himself on a legal rollercoaster with the next five years of his life at stake. Breaking the law is fairly straightforward, but trials are entirely unpredictable: they have their own language, rules, manipulations — and impact. Certain trials are remembered long after what caused them is forgotten. Beyond establishing their defense and avoiding or at least minimizing sentences, civil disobedients often use trials as a forum through which to publicize their motives. To pull that off takes a certain familiarity with the games of law, and for that reason the trial of Sam Lovejoy has become a primer in New Age legal consciousness.

Within a few hours after felling the tower, Sam was charged with "willful and malicious destruction of personal property," a felony entailing imprisonment of up to five years. He pleaded "absolutely not guilty" at the hearing and then won his first major battle when the judge freed him on a forum pro recognizance. Although many judges like to set high bail, the only legal purpose of bonding is to insure the defendant will show up to be tried. Since Sam had lived in the area all his life and had immediately turned himself in (with a written statement, no less) there wasn't much doubt that he intended to see the case through. Legally it was cut-and-dry, but veterans of the Franklin County Court System say the Lovejoy case was the first one in memory where the person being charged had bothered to read the bail statute, and that under normal circumstances there would have been a high price on Sam's body.

As it turned out, six months elapsed between the tower toppling and the trial, which gave Sam plenty of time to prepare his case. Determined to defend himself, Sam planned to base his case on the twin motives of self-preservation and community service. The charge against him was that he had destroyed the tower "willfully and maliciously." Sam argued that he hadn't acted "willfully," because "A nuke four miles from my house is like a gun four inches from my head. If someone stands there ready to kill you, defending yourself is hardly 'willful.' You don't really have any choice." As for the charge of malice, Lovejoy argued he had acted openly and in good faith, with no ill will toward any human. He had harmed no one and in fact had done something he felt was in the community's best interest. So where was the malice?

By the time the September 17 trial date rolled around, Lovejoy's head was packed with precedents and procedures. "The courts were a new trip for me," he says, "But I found it most intriguing. You'd be amazed at the number of linguistic mind games you can play. Of course, it all depends on exactly who it is you're playing them with."

Lovejoy had the good fortune to play them with Judge Kent B. Smith, generally known as one of the most liberal judges on the Massachusetts Superior Court Circuit. Smith had the patience and good faith to help Lovejoy in ways many other judges would not have.

A courtroom is geared for professionals who know the rules of the game. Lovejoy was a rank amateur, and in the early hours he showed it, continually making procedural errors, failing to file proper motions, stumbling over the subtleties of legalese. Time and again Smith would urge Lovejoy to get a lawyer, then demur and try to help Sam out. However much Smith might have preferred a lawyer-tailored defense, legally he had no choice but to accept Lovejoy's home-grown. The law provides that anyone wishing to conduct his or her own defense has that right.

The rule of thumb is that "anyone who acts as his own attorney has an idiot for a client," but for Lovejoy it was a matter of principle. "I wasn't about to pump any money into a lawyer or let the court appoint somebody I couldn't control. Besides that, I wanted to make a point. If the law is beyond the ability of the average citizen, then it isn't really law — it's just another prison."

Northeast Delaying Montague Nuke Project

Judge Lets Lovejoy Go Free

Greenfield Recorder
Sept. 26, 1974

Sam

Losing battle, but winning war

Since we published a cover story on Sam Lovejoy's Nuclear War (Oct. 18, 1974), the townspeople of western Massachusetts have had a chance to vote on a nuclear power referendum. The non-binding referendum, petitioned by the Alternative Energy Coalition (AEC), consisted of two yes-no questions: one registering opposition to the construction of the twin nuclear plants in Montague (where Lovejoy toppled the test tower); and a second, more radical question, which asked for the dismantling of two neighboring plants, one out of state in Vernon, Vt., and the other in Rowe, Mass.

While neither issue passed, Lovejoy's informants tell us that the 43-town district split pretty near down the middle on the first question: 22,962 against the Montague nukes; 25,622 for. The second question lost 2-1.

Undaunted, Lovejoy is said to have described the results "as a resounding victory for a spontaneous, common people's, grass roots movement."

"In the face of a combined annual utilities advertising budget of over $40 million," he said, "we spent about $3,000 and educated a hell of a lot of people about nuclear power. And those 32 percent who voted to dismantle the nukes—already existing plants worth over a billion dollars and generating what the government and utilities like to call 'much needed' electricity—those 15,000 people, are a die-hard opposition that isn't going to go away. I think the utilities are in trouble. I don't think the nukes will ever get built here."

AEC acts against atomic hijack

Without advance notice or publicity, the Atomic Energy Commission has recently posted stringent new regulations designed to spike what most people would dismiss as the scenario for an overly imaginative suspense thriller; namely, that terrorists might hijack a routine shipment of atomic material like enriched uranium 235 or

New Times
1974

Sam Lovejoy's "constituency" developed into the Alternative Energy Coalition (AEC)—a takeoff on the Atomic Energy Commission (AEC), the federal agency that regulates nuclear power plants. The AEC devised a number of well-chosen actions to develop enough grass-roots support to stop, possibly permanently, the nuclear power plant.

While opposition to the power plant was almost non-existent in early 1974, several months later the AEC canvassed and educated the public about the dangers of nuclear power, and by November 1974 they had filed petitions opposing nuclear power and gained enough support so that **48%** of local constituents opposed the construction of the Montague facility and **25%** were in favor of dismantling two existing nuclear power plants in other towns in Western Massachusetts. Continuing its organization on a more local level, the AEC, through successful warrants at town meetings, set up town energy conservation and alternative committees, and succeeded in getting town policy boards to disallow transportation and storage of nuclear waste.

Within four months of the '74 vote, the utilities postponed the building of the plant for four years, and because of continued and increased opposition to this and the Seabrook plant, have recently postponed the building of the plant another four years. It is doubtful the plant will be built.

CASE HISTORY #2: Mass. Fair Share

Mass Fair Share, Sept. 1977

After winning a suit against the city for the right to the list of tax delinquents, Mass Fair Share posted the list, including a list of the "dirty dozen plus two"—14 corporations and individuals who owed the city $4,258,686. Using plenty of media, it sent out "citizen tax bills," giving the delinquents several days to pay up. Many of them did, and those that didn't pay up immediately were unceremoniously visited by demonstrating Fair Share members. Within two weeks, $2.5 million had been returned to the city coffers.

The group received similar results when it pressured the city to go after a major airline which owed the city millions of dollars. It seemed that the airline executives disagreed with the reassessment rates levied by the city, and had paid only one half of what they owed for three years. Considering this a cheap way to get a cheap loan (interest charged on overdue taxes was 8%), Mass Fair Share claimed a coup when the airlines paid over $8.3 million before the end of the fiscal year.

CASE HISTORY #3: National United Church of Christ Office of Communication

"Standing" in Jackson, Mississippi

In 1964, however, when the Office of Communication of the United Church of Christ filed a petition to deny the license renewal of WLBT, a television station in Jackson, Mississippi, the FCC continued to insist that public groups were not "parties in interest." The Office of Communication had joined with local citizens in Jackson who charged that WLBT was guilty of racial and religious discrimination and of excessive commercialism.

The petitioners challenged the Commission's refusal to allow them to intervene; and in an historic opinion two years later, the U.S. Court of Appeals in the District of Columbia reversed the FCC ruling, and ordered that the petitioners be permitted to participate in a public hearing. The Jackson station eventually lost its license in 1969.

The FCC, as a result of the U.S. Court of Appeals decision in the WLBT case, could no longer claim that public groups had no "standing," were not "parties in interest."

It was a landmark decision, written for a unanimous three-judge court by Judge Warren E. Burger, who later became the Chief Justice of the United States. "We cannot believe," Judge Burger stated, "that the congressional mandate of public participation . . . was meant to be limited to writing letters to the Commission, to inspection of records, to the Commission's grace in considering listener claims, or to mere non-participating appearance at hearings . . .

When the license was revoked, the FCC agreed that a non-profit organization should conduct an interim operation of the station until a permanent applicant could qualify for the license.

About half the net profits derived from the interim operations of the station was allocated to the development of educational television; a communications training facility was set up at a predominantly black college; religious and racial discrimination vanished; a number of new shows produced and directed by blacks for the black community were established.

CASE HISTORY #4: The Lower East Side, New York

The Story of the USA's First Urban Solar System and Windmill

When a landlord abandons a building in New York, and fails to pay taxes on it for three years, the city takes over the property in a program called "in rem." Before a buyer comes along, the city can demolish the building. One needs only to walk through the Dresden's of the Lower East Side and the South Bronx to understand how common the occurrence is. Bulldozers have demolished entire blocks where poor people's communities once thrived.

519 E. 11th Street was slated for demolition, but after seeing the house, Freedberg and Landy decided they should save and restore the building—for reasons transcending the Switchboard's purposes. They should rebuild it as a symbol that poor people could fight back and retrieve their homes.

Committing themselves to the idea, Freedberg and Landy went to talk to activists on the Lower East Side. With their assistance, the pair mobilized a group of young Puerto Ricans interested in buying and co-oping the building.

WIN Magazine, Feb. 3, 1977

The results over the past few years have been the establishment of shared neighborhood solar and wind energy, a series of community gardens and coops (with plans for) distribution warehouses for the coops); housing coops, community controlled schools, and production of some of the same products that are now shipped into the community (at a cost of 67 cents per dollar for shipping and expensive packaging). And as people raise trout in their basements, grow food from hydroponic or community gardens, and set up a network of community coops, a greater percentage of money that once went to corporate interests now goes to the community.

WHAT ORGANIZATIONS GET FROM ACTION

- **Actions Bring Results:**

When effective, a strategy undertaken by a citizen group can force the existing structure to undergo enormous changes, such as the preceding case studies indicate. Sometimes change is slow and imperceptable, and many groups disintegrate because results are too long in coming. But action makes a push on the system and forces an immediate reaction, which often serves as a weathervane (as the song says): to see which way the wind blows.

- **Actions Bring Others Into the Organization:**

Action draws attention to an issue: it makes some people aware (or reminded) of the problem; it gets many people stirred up; it shows people that you're a group that's making itself heard. Action, then, brings people into the organization at three levels:

1. *Membership increases.* When Sam Lovejoy toppled the tower membership increased in the AEC from roughly 30 people to over 100; the community development projects in New York City have resulted in vastly increased participation in community projects.

2. *Support increases.* In a town vote, nearly half the county opposed the nuclear power plant.

3. *Coalitions are built.* The Jacksonville Coalition had to enlist the aid of other groups in the community before it won its case; the AEC got the help of "less radical" energy concern groups—ecology and conservation groups within the system—thereby improving credibility in the community.

- **Action Affects Power Relationships:**

Most people are powerless because of the manipulative power of a few. Effective action can redistribute that power to citizens. It can give people control over production, housing, economic development, jobs, utility rates and the media.

- **Action Can Cause Broader Changes in the Community:**

First, it *raises the consciousness of the public:* the entire community is affected when one portion of the system is altered or challenged. The changes brought about in TV programming in Jacksonville no doubt affected everyone who watched the station. The model of self-sufficiency and economic independence which the New York City neighborhood provides other low-income neighborhoods cannot help but influence and pave the way for future endeavors.

Secondly, it *can build a movement:* the AEC has not only delayed the Montague nuclear power plant so far, it has also helped thousands of people explore alternative sources of energy and self-sufficient lifestyles. Over 2000 people rallied to stop the Seabrook nuclear power plant; the occupation attracted support and created movements throughout the country.

Finally, it *can provide incentive for other groups:* it's always good for morale for anyone working for social change to read about another community organization's victory or success. Sometimes it can energize and inspire members of a dragging organization to keep going. A success for one can be considered a success for all; especially if the organizer seizes the opportunity.

POSSIBLE PROBLEMS

1. You may lose: The result of your action may favor the other side. For most organizations, losses are salvageable; some losses can even turn out to be victories. But some losses are devastating and may mark the end of some peoples' commitment to social change (evidence the droves of prople who dropped out of the protest movements of the 60s after the marches and moratoriums in Washington went unheeded by President Nixon).

The best way to avoid this kind of loss is to scrutinize consciously each course of action and contingency plan. Be aware of all the consequences of any action. Obviously, if the actions are going to hurt you more than they will help, don't do it. But this isn't always very easy to foresee:

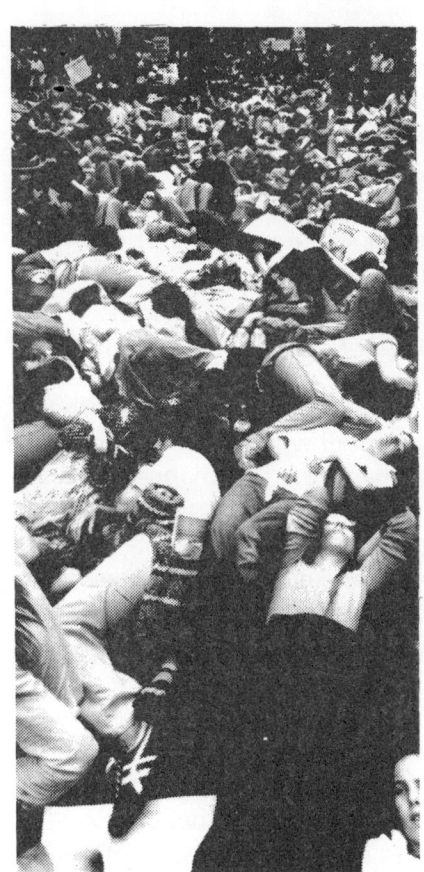
Lionel Delevingne

> Some people were thinking about forcing the issue the next day by sitting down and blocking the access road the next morning, when police and officials would try to drive through. They argued that we were playing into the authorities hands by complying so readily to their rules and by allowing them to come and go through our ranks at any hour of the day or night.
>
> We had come knowing we might get arrested. But did we have to actually get arrested in order to be successful?
>
> The camp was divided. Some thought a small confrontation might be misconstrued by the police and would incite tear gas, clubbings and confusion. Those who favored the action felt that if the arrests didn't start until Monday or Tuesday, there would be fewer people to arrest and would therefore have less impact.
>
> Luckily for us, the decision never had to be reached. Governor Thompson arrived on the site just then and informed us we would be arrested if we did not leave. A cheer rang through the camp. Governor Thompson did not know what a savior he had been.
>
> —From **Seabrook: From the Inside (A Protestor's Journal)**; Springfield Morning Union, May 16, 1977.

The best way is to have everyone own the decision for action. Discussing possible consequences—including the possibility of loss—ahead of time helps people to see the action as part of an on-going struggle and minimizes the negative reactions when instant victory isn't achieved.

2. You may lose numbers: This can happen when you win as well as when you lose: an organizer's Catch 22. It is fairly obvious why people drop out after a loss. One reason people leave when they win is because they think they got what they wanted—they think the problem's solved—and they therefore feel they don't need the organization anymore. After members of the National Welfare Rights Organization were able to secure clothing and furniture allowances for their constituents, the constituents left the organization satisfied, before deeper issues—like why welfare recipients have to fight to obtain what is legally theirs—were explored. At the same time, people need to satisfy their immediate needs (fill their stomachs) before they'll take on something more risky and seemingly abstract.

Organizers should be aware of what the community values as victories and think of the consequences of those victories. This can be undermined some by insuring that the group identifies root causes from the onset. Another helpful measure is to see to it that a series of shorter term, small victories can be achieved so that members see the process as a long journey with several milestones along the way.

3. You/the group may be co-opted: This usually happens when you are offered a certain type of concession. *Is the offer beneficial to the "other side?" Will it allow the other side more long-range control over you or the issue?* The more you know of the opponent and what it has to offer, the better chance you may have to plan a non-co-optable strategy.

4. You may not be able to agree on strategy: One of the most aggravating situations to be in is to spend hour after hour of meeting time debating, vacillating, and getting nowhere. There will be those who favor conservative, intermediary measures and those who want to blow things wide open.

Unless the organizer can help the group to clarify its goals and objectives and to evaluate all action in the light of these goals, the group may defeat itself before ever planning the action.

5. You've decided to take the action, but now not enough people will take part in it: Then don't do it.

6. You want to do it yourself: always a temptation. If this is so, try asking yourself some of the basic questions about why you are involved in social change and what you expect to get out of it at the beginning of this manual.

ACTION: VARIOUS APPROACHES

Alinsky — Style Organizing	Mandated Citizen Participation Organizing:
Alinsky organizing is characterized by large numbers of people using confrontation tactics. The assumption here is that numbers can offset the power and resources of the enemy. The group selects or *polarizes* the enemy, *isolates* the one key person who can best deal with the problem. (All others are ignored.) Demands are often written up and presented to the enemy with a threat. Unless the demands are met (or unless a promise to meet the demands is signed) further action is taken. Using this model, tenants might hold a rent strike until the landlord makes repairs in a building; a consumer group might withhold payment on electric bills until electric rates are reduced. **Some questions this approach raises include:** • *Are we acting merely for the sake of acting, or will we gain some power from this action?* • *Will our tactics alienate those we want to influence and do more detriment than good?* • *Are we prepared for and committed to the consequences we have stated if the demands are not met?* • *Are we prepared for a struggle, or are we a short-term group?* • *Are we prepared to follow-up if we lose the first round?*	In this instance action usually takes the form of a public campaign or set of recommendations intended to force the appropriate government agency to change policy. Because members of the group usually cannot afford to lose their credibility with people they are trying to influence, the mandated group's approach is essentially a media campaign and public awareness-raising approach (debates, hearings, forums, speakers, pamphlets, petitions, etc). Some examples of this approach include: a regional Title XX group attempting to change policy regarding confidentiality of records by confronting state and federal officials through legal and policy-making channels; a Council for Children initiating a letter-writing and media campaign to the state legislature to lobby for more health services for physically handicapped children; a Welfare Advisory Board attending hearings and contacting administrators and legislators to secure better services for battered wives. **Questions this approach raises include:** • *Can we really make a difference? How much of a difference will our action make?* • *Will the action we take actually solve the* cause *of the problem, or just a* symptom *of the problem?* • *Can we protect ourselves from being co-opted?* • *Are we fulfilling our mandate? Is our mandate designed to get at symptoms only?* • *What do we risk by challenging our mandate?*

Public Advocacy Organizing:	Community Control Approach:	Consciousness-Raising Approach:
Generally, action is determined by the organizers; major strategies include lobbying, public advocacy, petitioning, survey and poll-taking, public hearings, and confrontation when necessary. Some examples of this approach include: a Public Interest Research Group (PIRG) writing a bottle bill, educating the public about the bill through the media and encouraging other individuals and groups to support the bill; a state-wide health group training people to be able to force hospitals to provide free health care for low income residents.	Here action takes the form of building alternatives...setting up new models and institutions which work to alleviate the problem. This method employs collaborative strategies rather than confrontation or campaigning to build that alternative. Where action in the Alinsky approach is usually reactive (we'll do this to stop the bulldozers from destroying our community) the Community Control approach is proactive ("together we can build community housing"). Some examples of this approach include: a neighborhood group running a food co-op; a number of mothers running their own day care center; workers running a community-run business.	While this approach is often eclectic, there has been a tendency for consciousness-raising groups to develop alternative cultural and economic programs as a way to support and act on the awareness that members have been developing, and to confront sources of oppression through strikes, sit-ins, and economic boycotts. Some examples of this approach include: a woman's group that decides to establish a counseling center for women who want to begin to become more self-sufficient; a group of workers that realizes through discussion and analysis that they must begin to control their own workplace in order to feel good about their work; a group of students who decide to establish an alternative high school in order to take control of their own learning.

Questions this approach raises include: (Public Advocacy Organizing)

- Are we allowing low-income people, working class and minorities to have say in our actions? How?

- Are we turning the wrong people off by our actions?

- Is the action appropriate for the necessary level of change? (Taking over a building when traditional channels haven't been exhausted yet may draw more criticism and alienation from the media and the public than it does good; on the other hand, it may be apparent that traditional channels aren't working and wouldn't work.)

- Are our actions dealing with symptoms or causes of our problems?

Questions this approach raises include: (Community Control)

- Do we have enough resources to develop and continue our project?

- Are we really helping the community with this project? What/who is being developed?

- Can it be done?

- What major difficulties will we encounter? How can they be anticipated and dealt with?

- What skills will people need to acquire? How?

"Mass-Based Organizing:"

Mass-Based organizers have used an Alinsky-style approach, but because they are normally a state-based organization, they are often able to affect larger, state-wide issues, because they are not limited to neighborhood issues.

This approach raises the same questions as the Alinsky-style approach.

Questions this approach raises include: (Consciousness-Raising)

- Are we organizing and empowering people or are we "servicing" people?

- Do we have enough resources to be successful in our action?

- Are we being clear with the public about the motivations for our action?

- Will the public be supportive or threatened?

VISION: A SOCIAL CHANGE PERSPECTIVE

When we talk of social change, most organizers agree that we are talking about planned, purposeful change. Three words come to mind: a *vision* of a better world; some *goals* to begin to achieve the vision; and *action*—something we can do right now to achieve our goals and begin to realize that vision.

Martin Luther King and many of those working in the civil rights movement were experts in the use of action to achieve goals and work toward a vision. They successfully used boycotts and marches, among other things, to integrate public transportation in Memphis and elsewhere and gain the right to vote for blacks. The specific actions were well organized, and for the most part, examples of superb community organization. But these actions didn't happen in isolation from one another. They were part of a larger goal, that of integration, equal rights and dignity and respect for black people. . . a goal that allowed King and other civil rights leaders to pick and choose actions for effectiveness.

But much of King's success came not only because of what he was able to mobilize in the South, but because of the support he had gained from northerners, support he was able to gain as he literally shared his vision—most notably his "I Have a Dream" speech.

King's actions, then, were not random or reactive or done merely to provide small- or medium-sized victories. Like others who have created long-range change, King's actions were part of larger, longer-range goals and visions and were determined and evaluated by those goals.

Determining actions from visions and goals can help the community organizer in the following ways:

1. It provides organizations with a purpose, a reason for being.

2. It can help people choose which actions to take and *how* to implement these actions.

3. It brings people into an organization and keeps people in that organization. Many can agree on a purpose, even when they do not agree on a specific action.

4. It provides a way to plan for the future, a direction; and a way to evaluate the past.

The purpose of this exercise is to help an organization think of broad purposes or visions, more specific goals, and see how specific action options fit into these goals and visions. Fill out the diagram below by answering the following questions.

1. Problem: *What is the problem with which you are dealing?* Include as part of the problem the root cause.

2. Vision: *What is the ideal situation you are working toward?* Visions are ideals and can be as far reaching as reality permits.

—*How would people relate to each other in this ideal situation?*
—*How would resources be allocated in this ideal situation?*

Note: If you filled out the questions in the Introduction, you have already answered these questions.

3. Goals: *What specific goals would help you reach the vision?* Goals should be measurable and specific. They might be things like a food co-op, a new library, a worker controlled factory.

4. Actions: *What actions will you need to achieve your goals?* An action may be a program or series of programs, a project, or an event. It too should be measurable and very specific. Actions may be a series of community meetings, a fund-raising drive, or a successful demonstration.

Each horizontal line on the diagram indicates one set of actions you may need to achieve the goal.

PROBLEM:	ACTIONS: ←	GOAL: ←	VISION:
	ACTIONS:	GOAL:	
ROOT CAUSES:	ACTIONS:	GOAL:	
	ACTIONS:	GOAL:	

MATCHING ACTION WITH LEVELS OF RESISTANCE

Lionel Delevingne

Focus on the specific actions that you listed in the preceeding diagram. Whatever they may be, you want those actions to be successful, and planning for success is called strategizing.

Strategizing becomes the nuts-and-bolts work of the community organizer. Like the daily encounters of any long-range journey, it requires extensive knowledge of a situation (who or what you're dealing with), and flexible use of strategies and tactics. Unfortunately, too many groups limit themselves to the use of one or two strategies. It helps to be aware of the variety of strategies and tactics before you decide on one. It also helps to have alternatives.

Roland Warren, social change theorist and author of **Studying Your Community** and **Peace, Love, and Social Change** has come up with a method of viewing strategy based on the amount of agreement or disagreement one finds in a situation.

The level of agreement/disagreement (what Warren calls consensus-disensus) between your group and those you have to deal with in a situation may be seen as a continuum, where there is a high level of agreement on the left, a medium level of possibility in the middle, and no possibility of agreement on the right.

Fully Agree |--------------------------| Fully Disagree

The level of agreement/disagreement should determine the type of solution that you'll use. Warren calls strategies where agreement is probable **collaborative strategies**; where agreement is probable, **campaign strategies**; and where agreement is impossible and competition must be pursued, **contest strategies**.

Collaborative Strategies:

Collaborative strategies are based on the assumption that two or more groups hold common values and interests, which would allow for agreement on proposals of action.

The predominant role of the organizer or change agent is that of an "enabler" or "catalyst." She is not concerned with putting through her own preconceived proposal, but with helping the groups involved reach consensus on the issue.

It is assumed that any differences are caused by misinformation or poor communication, so appropriate action calls for getting the facts and reconciling differing points of view on the basis of discussion and information. The chief obstacle is not opposition but rather, if anything, apathy and inaction.

Campaign Strategies:

This approach applies to situations where there is lack of agreement among principal parties whether an issue exists or how it should be resolved, but there is a likely prospect of reaching agreement.

The organizer's role is one of "translator"—he presents the problem in ways which can be understood to several different parties, implying that disagreement over the issue is merely superficial, and that the proposal actually does correspond to the "opposition's" basic values and interests.

Examples may involve mass media "educational" campaigns, letters, endorsements and the organization of ad hoc groups in order to direct attention or to promote the issue. In this case the organizers are trying to win over the parties by persuasion.

Courtesy Valley Advocate

Contest Strategies:

In this case there is gaping disagreement over the issue. Contest strategies involve pursuing one's own goal in opposition to others, if it is to be pursued at all.

The organizer's role is that of "contestant."

Contest strategies are characterized by the abandonment (temporarily at least) of efforts at consensus, and the employment of efforts to further one's own side of an issue despite opposition.

There is a tendency to equate all issue disensus situations with "conflict" strategies.

Four specific types of contest processes may be identified:

1. A contest of opposing positions within accepted social norms for the resolution of a problem.

2. A contest set up to alter the distribution of power in the community.

3. A contest of opposing positions in violation of usual social norms. (One or more parties break the rules in order to resolve the issue in their favor. This situation most often develops around new leaders or groups who have fewer attachments to the community and are less likely to support the rules according to which community affairs are generally conducted, e.g.: anti-flouridation groups, rent strikes, welfare rights organizations, anti-segregation groups. Civil disobedience is often the mechanism used.)

4. A contest to attempt deliberately to harm the opponent or remove him from the field of the issue. This is conflict in the strict sense of the word, e.g.: attempting to depose a particular official, to destroy a career, or to bankrupt a firm, using various types of harassment, physical violence.

Combinations of Strategies:

It is important to remember that issue resolution often requires a combination of strategies, and a change effort could run from a period of a few weeks to a few years. As the issue develops, different types of situations may characterize it along the dimension of issue consensus-disensus. There may also be times when specific action episodes may also render distinct characteristics.

Constantly re-evaluating the nature of the situation permits us to apply a number of strategies to an issue as the situation surrounding it develops and changes.

Lionel Delevingne

COLLABORATIVE STRATEGIES

When to use it...

• We're confident we can reach agreement now or after full discussion

• We have a common interest

• We have common values

• The problem between our groups is misinformation and mis-communication

• We are sure that there is no major value or conflict of interest between us

Possible actions...

• Fact-finding

• Clearing up misunderstandings

• Clearing up differences through meetings, newsletters, fact sheets

• Forming coalitions (on-going or ad hoc)

• Setting up interpersonal dynamics training sessions (T-groups, communication workshops)

• Setting up educational workshops

Roles of the Organizers...

• Enablers

• Catalysts

• Educators

• Liaisons

• Facilitators

CAMPAIGN STRATEGIES

When to use it...

• We don't have agreement, but expect to get it

• We can convince them that "our" proposal conforms to their "true" values or interests

• We can avoid their active antagonism and opposition

Possible actions...

• Attempt to gain agreement through educational campaigns:
    mass media
    testimonials
    organizing ad hoc groups
    endorsements

Roles of the Organizers...

• Translators

• Persuaders, through pressure, inducements (votes, money, favors, etc.)

• Bargainers

CONFRONTATION STRATEGIES

When to use it...

• We'll never get agreement through explicit statements or discussion

• They refuse to recognize our issues

• They oppose our position/proposal

• They only stand to lose if we get what we want

Possible actions...

• Go over, under, around and through any effective oppositions or deterrent through:
    debates
    strikes
    pickets
    deposing officials
    harassment
    boycotting

Roles of the Organizers...

• Contestants

• Spokespersons

• Cheerleaders/Coaches

• Risk-takers

• Participants

• Co-strategizers

Now let's work on strategy, keeping in mind the different types of strategy available to you. Fill out the following diagram:

A.	B.	C.	D.
Name(s) of who it is you want to change.	What do you want the person(s) to do and *by when?* (Prioritize.)	Actions which would get what you want from them.	Predictable consequences of each of these actions. (Which are the most meaningful? Which are easiest?) Prioritize and compare to Column B.

STRATEGY CHECKLISTS

Different sets of criteria are required for each of the three strategies that we have discussed. The rest of this chapter consists of checklists for each of the three strategies. Decide which strategy you will be using, and go over the appropriate checklist. Good luck in your action!

Lionel Delevingne

COLLABORATIVE STRATEGIES

Collaboration means working together. People and groups work together when they recognize mutual needs and recognize that working together will help them meet those needs better than working alone. Collaborative strategies have *brought key people into community organizations;* they have brought community organizations together to form *coalitions;* these strategies have brought key members, groups, and/or coalitions together to form *movements.* Labor unions, the women's movement, the alternative education/youth culture movement, the black movement, hispanic movement and movement of the elderly all began when people realized that they had a lot in common with each other, and began to build that commonality into organization, and in many cases, into culture.

But not all coalitions are or have to be long-range. Many people view coalitions as temporary organizations, from which a smaller organization can borrow power.

No matter why you choose the collaborative strategy, you have felt that it will get you further than confronting a group, and you realize that it isn't necessary to campaign a group. Here are some questions to ask yourself to make sure this approach will work for you.

(CHECKLIST: Collaborative Strategies)

1. Will it get you where you want to go? Some people use collaborative strategies merely because they don't like to campaign or confront. Others see it as a way of expanding contacts or socializing. As a result, the collaboration may take on no political significance.

• What will you get from the collaboration?

• How do you know that you'll get it?

2. Can you mix work with pleasure in a way which adds to the cause? Even though real social change should be viewed as a struggle, there is no reason why there shouldn't be elements of fun in the struggle. Social events may provide the perfect vehicle for change; at minimum they can help keep members from burning-out. The Seabrook Occupiers held an Occupier's Ball on the first anniversary of the demonstration and seized the opportunity to bring people back together, rekindle the spirit of community and solidarity and to share new anti-nuke songs, poems, plays and information. The event also served to get people together just before the next serious action; the lightheartedness of the ball made the seriousness of the issues easier to cope with.

• When might a party be appropriate?

• Is it possible to plan activities (dances, dinners, picnics, talent shows) to help reach the goals?

• Is there a symbolic event we can use as an excuse to get people together in a celebrative way?

3. Are there special ways to reach the person or group that you want to reach? In many situations, a few key decision-makers can sway the others in the group. If you can reach these key decision-makers, you may save yourself some time and energy.

Lionel Delevingne

• Who needs to agree to the collaboration, and through what mechanism? Executive board? Executive Director? Chairperson? Committee? Entire group? Consensus? Majority vote? Executive action?

• Will it help to speak to a few key people in the group first, to begin to lay the groundwork? (Who are they? How can you best get to them? Are you sure that going this route won't cause problems (ignoring hierarchy, etc.)? What special information will this person need?)

4. Is the media being used as well as it might be?* Any organizer will tell you of the crucial role the media can play in an organizing effort. Positive or even neutral media coverage has provided many a group with the public support or the illusion of support to win many gains in the past.

• What kinds of media problems might your group have?

• Is the group aware of the prejudices and policies of the individuals who determine local media coverage?

Lionel Delevingne

	Article	Coverage	Editorial	Feature	PSA	Photo	Interview Show
Radio Stations (list)							
TV Stations (list)							
Newspapers (list)							
Newsletters (list)							

*NOTE: For more information, see the C!TP manual on using the media

- Are you able to meet the media's needs for objectivity as well as its needs for the "scoop"?

- Are there media people whose "beat" covers your issues and concerns? Do you have access to them? Who are they?

- Are media spokespeople designated? Are others in the group prepared to speak to the media knowledgeably, without endangering the reputation of the organization? Are there things you don't want people to say? Do they know this? Do they know why?

- Has the group sat down and written out a list of goals and objectives for media exposure e.g. We would like to see the issue covered in a weekly series, editorials, PSAs, etc.)?

- Has the group devised appropriate media strategies to meet these goals?

- Do members of the group know the basics of writing press releases, PSAs, etc., so that all the work doesn't fall on a few?

- When are local newspaper, radio and TV deadlines?

- Is coverage timing important? Is there a need for a media person to be present at a certain moment (e.g. during a walkout) and can the media be there then?

- Have you prepared a press packet (of news releases, background information, contact people) for each of the expected media representatives?

- Is a press conference appropriate? Who would be the spokesperson? (spokespeople?)

- How about other types of media (handouts and flyers, t-shirts, banners, bumper stickers, posters, etc.)?

- Has the group assessed its past media experience and success? Are there additional strategies you haven't tried that would be more effective (e.g. using video)?

- Has the group critiqued its own PR (brochures, press releases, etc.)? Why didn't that last press release get picked up by many local papers?

5. Will you need alliances in order to get what you want? Working with other groups can pose problems as well as bring about benefits. The other group(s) may operate under a different set of values, they may have different work styles, or they may not want the same results that you want from an action.

- What kinds of support problems might the group have?

- Is association with some group going to develop credibility gap between negotiators and the constituency?

- Does the group have the leadership which can accomplish the tasks involved? What work is involved?

- Do you have groups that will work with you? Which ones do you need? Why might they work with you (or not work with you)?

- Do we have the resources to become involved in policy-making, or will the other group(s) "take over" leadership?

Community Union Newsletter

6. Have you dealt with maintenance problems you might have? So far, questions have dealt with those outside of your group: other groups, the media, etc. Now it is time to take a look at how well those within your organization can function in their attempt to work on the action and issues.

- What kinds of problems does the structure of the organization pose?

- What kind of leadership style does the group have?

7. Do you need to practice the action before you do it? If you have finished this set of questions and still feel somewhat unsure of your ability to be successful, try role-playing the situation, then diagnose the problems and brainstorm solutions.

To do the role-play, identify all the major "actors" and "actresses" (including your group). Spend some time reviewing what you know of each "character" before you role-play. The more accurate the role-play, the more you will learn from it.

After the role-play, try asking the questions to the right.

- What kind of spokespeople will be needed?

- Can the leadership maintain "staying power" within the larger negotiating group?

- Is the group cohesive enough?

- Will contact with certain groups develop a credibility gap between the leader(s) and other members of the group? What are the implications of this?

- Did the role-play reproduce the issues we will probably be faced with?

- What problems were identified in the role-play? (be specific).

- What can we do about these problems?

- What did it feel like to be the opposition? What were their fears, needs, issues, etc.?

CAMPAIGN STRATEGIES

While campaigning strategies have traditionally been used to persuade key individuals or organizations to join in on a specific action, they have been increasingly used to hold elected officials, bureaucrats or corporations accountable to specific citizen needs. In either case, campaign strategies mean working to some degree in someone else's system, something many community organizations have not been interested in doing because it may "cloud the issues" or co-opt the community organization. But skeptics should be aware of the possibilities of this approach before canning the idea. Some recent examples of effective use of this strategy follow.

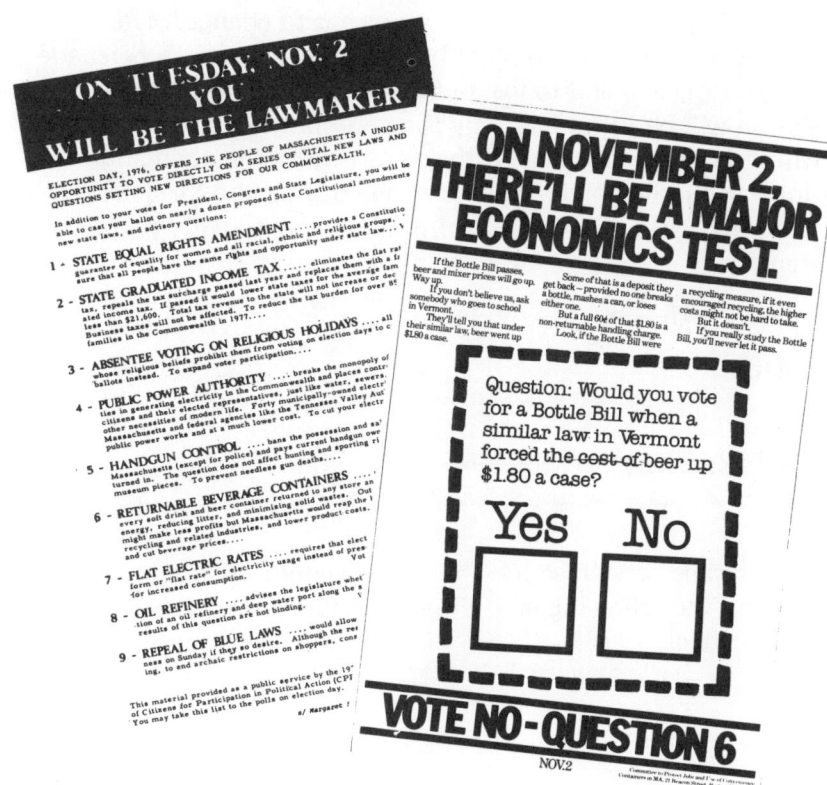

By law, there are over 200 **Health Planning Councils** across the country. These councils are mandated to be governed by boards of directors, at least 50% of which must be considered "consumers"— citizens not related to the health-care profession. Thus the ordinary citizen can be well represented. The citizen council has sign-off powers—must give authorization—on any federal or state health or mental health monies (over $100,000), be it a hospital, expensive equipment, or what have you. Citizen health-care advocates see this law as insuring that health-care providers spend money on facilities and equipment that will benefit the general public.

• **The Mitchell Transfer Amendment** has attempted, for the past several years, to take 12 billion from what some elected officials call military waste (support of dictatorships, military personnel efficiencies, cost over-runs) and put that money into human needs spending. It is expected that the amendment will take several years of campaigning, debating and support before enough congressmen will pass it. Nevertheless, it is the first time that any group has made a significant attack on military spending. Tactics include massive letter-writing, demonstrations (such as picketing and leafleting post offices on tax-return deadline day to inform the public where tax funds go), securing local support, rallies, slide shows, etc.

• **National Peoples Action (NPA)**, a coalition of grass-roots groups from at least 100 cities across the country, has done a great deal to make the issue of red-lining a major national concern, and has successfully pushed for the passage of the Community Re-Investment Act, a bill that requires banks to demonstrate that they serve the convenience and needs (including the loan needs) of the communities in which they are chartered to do business. The bill further states that banks have an *affirmative obligation* to meet the credit needs of local communities.

NPA holds its 2500 member annual convention in Washington, D.C., where its members have access to key national decision-makers. When the 2500 members aren't strongly pressuring key administration officials, they break into small groups to lobby with their hometown Senators and Representatives.

(CHECKLIST: Campaign Strategies)

1. Are you clear about what or who you want to change? The following forms should help you plan the process necessary to persuade an individual or group and to insure that a policy change or piece of legislation will be followed up by the appropriate people. The latter will require a knowledge of the steps involved in changing legislation. Such information can be attained from the League of Women Voters, various manuals, or from individuals who "know the system."

STRATEGIES NECESSARY TO PERSUADE AN INDIVIDUAL OR GROUP

I. We want to persuade _____
to _____ by _____

II. They would be persuaded by or affected by the following incidents (prioritize):
1.
2.
3.
4.
5.

III. We could use our strengths and resources to persuade them in the following ways:
1.
2.
3.
4.
5.

IV. The following would be the easiest and most effective approaches that our group could use (rank):

Easy to do	Effective	
_____	_____	Television interview/news
_____	_____	Television Public Service Announcement (PSA)
_____	_____	Radio news
_____	_____	Radio PSA
_____	_____	Radio talk show
_____	_____	Newspaper advertising
_____	_____	Newspaper article
_____	_____	Testimonial by_____ saying _____
_____	_____	Endorsement by_____ saying _____
_____	_____	Brochure (What must it say?)
_____	_____	Flyer (What must it say?)
_____	_____	Coercion (Which tactic?)
_____	_____	Bargaining (We have the following to offer them:_____) (We have the following to threaten them:_____)
		Other: _____

- What resources does the group have to persuade the individual or group?

- Which tactics would the individual or group respond to?

- Are you clear on the steps necessary for persuasion?

- Is what you want the individual or group to be persuaded about clear in your minds? How will you know you have succeeded (what actions or events will indicate to you that they have been persuaded?)

- Does the group fully understand all the mechanisms, structures, processes and pressures the individual or group you want to persuade is working within?

- Step (state what each step entails) _____
- To be done by _____ (key person or group)
- Date to be done _____
- To be monitored by _____ (person from your group)

2. Will it get you what you want? A little projecting into the future to play out all the possible outcomes of an action (or set of actions) can help you decide whether your tactics will, in fact, lead the appropriate person(s) to respond the way you'd like, or whether your actions might boomerang, or be misinterpreted. Although the Clamshell Alliance was extremely careful to be in contact with police and state authorities concerning their plans for the occupation (to the point of making access routes known, sharing all training literature with the police and publishing occupation guidelines in the media), the Governor still seized the opportunity to plant rumors in the media that the Clam was a group of violent agitators. As the occupation progressed, the media focused less on the non-violent aspect of the occupation and more on the tremendous financial burden the protestors were costing the state of New Hampshire, thereby shifting the focus from the issue of nuclear power to the controversy of civil disobedience and the cost of protesting on the people of the state.

• *Is there a chance your actions will be misinterpreted? Can you anticipate/avoid this somehow?*

• *How will you know you've gotten what you want? (What are the indicators?)*

• *Have you prepped group members about how to give interviews to the media (what not to say and what to say)? Are media spokespeople designated and trained?*

• *Are you 'barking up the wrong tree?'*

3. Have you focused your action? Some groups make a big mistake by diffusing their actions and resources over many targets. Accomplishing this kind of change requires clear-cut targets and consolidated efforts (in terms of energy and resources).

• *Can you do all you've set out to do (in the amount of time you have to do it in)?*

• *Are group members unified in opinion and willing to stick together to bring pressure to bear?*

• *Is there more than one target? Will that divide your resources?*

• *Do all group members fully understand the goals, the indicators of success and the eventual change the group is working toward? Do group members see how they fit into that?*

4. Can you sustain the action until you get what you want? The organizers of the Clamshell Alliance informed the people who planned to occupy the nuclear power plant site that they expected the stint in jail to last only one night. It was 15 days before negotiations were finally reached. Many people were not prepared for such a long stay and had to return home to their children and jobs before negotiations were finished. But enough people had been prepared so that they could hold out long enough to win an acceptable release. In the case of confrontation, the opposition usually plays the waiting game—how long can you hold out and maintain solidarity and morale (since time is usually on the opposition's side)?

• *How long will it take?*

• *Are members prepared (physically, psychologically, economically)?*

• *What resources are needed?*

• *What can be done to sustain membership involvement and avoid drop-outs, burn-outs, and loss of morale?*

- *Is there a mechanism to support those who cannot stay with the action (to maintain solidarity)?*

- *Are there contingency plans so the group won't fall apart if the battle goes on longer than expected?*

5. Have you underestimated who you are working with? If the person you are negotiating with is a businessman, politician or agency official, he probably got there because of his ability to negotiate. When he starts using technical language or bureaucratese, ask him to break it down into simple English. Will he meet your demands? If not, what, specifically, is his position? You need to know, so you can tell the group. They have sent you to find out what his position is.

If the person you're negotiating with tries to throw you off the track, just ask him very slowly, "What will you do about our *demands*?"

A good example of this way of responding to the "opposition" was used by a small rural community which was about to lose its neighborhood health clinic. The County Health Department sent a man down to the local community center to try to explain why the clinic had been removed without consulting with the community. It was a large turnout, and the Health Department man explained and explained. Finally he said, "Are there any questions?"

- *Are you familiar with how the "opposition" operates?*

- *Are you familiar with the "opposition's" rhetoric? Will someone who can "translate" what is being said for the group be present to interpret and ask probing questions (or, has that skill been passed on to others in the group)?*

- *How do members of the group respond to authority? Are they easily intimidated or smoke-screened? Has the group discussed each individual's response to the "opposition"?*

A woman in the back of the room stood up and said slowly, "Why are you taking the clinic?"

The Health Department man explained for about ten more minutes. Then he asked if there were any other questions.

Then a man stood up and said very slowly, "Why are you taking the clinic?"

This went on for about an hour before the Health Department man realized that he could not smoke-screen the group with diplomacy.

6. Is the media being used as well as it might be? (see Collaborative Strategy Checklist, Question 4.)

7. Will you need alliances in order to get what you want? (See Collaborative Strategy Checklist, Question 5.)

8. Do you need practice before taking action? (See Collaborative Strategies Checklist, Question 7.)

CONFRONTATION STRATEGIES

Confrontation strategy is a strategy of last resort. Some organizers feel that group should not confront another person or group until all else fails. The chances for public support are shakiest when a group must confront, and public support is vital to a financially-powerless group. The other side of the coin is that the most significant victories of community organizations have come about by use of this strategy.

*Poor People's Movements—Why They Succeed, How They Fail, by Frances Fox Piven and Richard A. Cloward; Pantheon Books, New York, 1977.

For most organizations, such an approach leaves the "opposition" with three responses: they can *ignore* you, they can *punish* you, or they can *placate* you. The strength of and outside support for your group, as well as the type of demands that your group makes will determine which response the opposition will choose.

Piven and Cloward* take a long, critical look at these responses and at short-, medium-, and long-range consequences of political disruption in their book **Poor Peoples's Movements**. They measure change not in terms of the disruption of public institutions, rather, in terms of the political impact of the disruptions. During normal periods, political leaders can either ignore or repress protest movements. But when protest movements arise a period arises which gives the poor hope and makes political leaders somewhat vulnerable, so that they cannot ignore disturbances or employ punitive measures. The only option left is to placate.

Piven and Cloward see placating as taking several forms:

Concessions are offered to remedy immediate, symbolic and tangible grievances (the right to relief in the 30s; the right to desegregate public facilities in the 60s). Such reform requires a break with established patterns of government, and it is here where the poor make their gains.

Political leaders try to quiet disturbances by attempting to channel energies and angers of the protestors into more "legitimate" and "less disruptive" forms of behavior, through co-optation (establishing welfare grievance procedures, 'advisory' committees, dialogues between both sides, etc.).

Government measures are used to undermine whatever sympathy the group has been able to command from a wide public (Social Security instead of the Townsend plan, the War on Poverty and Model Cities to appease blacks and white liberals, etc.).

Apparently conciliatory measures make it possible for the government to safely employ repressive measures as well. Leaders are harrassed and arrested (Martin Luther King, anti-war groups, etc.).

Lionel Delevingne

This process, the shift from protest to pacification, proves the demise of protest, not only because it co-opts leaders, but because it transforms the political climate which makes protest possible. Concessions to the protestors create a powerful image of a benevolent and responsive government. Support from the larger population dwindles and triggers the antagonistic sentiments of more neutral sectors.

The residue of reform that is left is that which turns out to be compatible (or at least not incompatible) with the interests of the economic groups who currently have control.

Listed below are some of the typical responses made by power structures. Be prepared for all of them.

• *Symbolic Satisfactions* (the appearance of action, such as walking tours, ribbon-cutting ceremonies, expensive studies, lots of rhetoric rather than allocations or innovations which could really make a difference).

• The other side may dispense *token material satisfactions*, while appearing to make a difference by responding to the demands. The other side may be only responding on a case-by-case basis. In the handling of crisis cases, public officials give the appearance of responding to their reference publics, while mitigating demands for an expensive, complex general assault on problems represented by the cases to which responses are given.

Token responses, whether or not accompanied by more general responses, are particularly attractive to reporters who are able to dramatize individual cases convincingly, but may be unable to capture the essence of general suffering.

• The other side may *organize internally in order to blunt the impetus* of the protest efforts. They may be able to handle the worst cases, pre-empting protest efforts by responding to cases which best dramatize protest demands. Does the other side's response get to the root causes of the problems?

• The other side *may appear to be constrained in their ability to grant protest goals.* They may try to make the protestors appear unreasonable, or well-meaning individuals who "just don't understand the complexity of the situation." They may claim to lack resources and/or authority, or may evade the protest demands by arguing that, "If I give it to you, I have to give it to everyone."

• The other side may use their extensive resources to *discredit* protest leaders and organizations. Utilizing their excellent access to the press, they may say that the group or its leaders are ineffective, unreliable, don't have the people behind them, etc. There may or may not be truth to their allegations.

• The other side may *postpone action.* The effect of this, if accompanied by symbolic assurances, is to remove immediate pressure and delay specific commitments to a future date. This is usually effective because of pressure group inherent instability. The most frequent method for postponing is to commit a subject to further study.

(CHECKLIST: Confrontation Strategies)

1. Is the action significant enough to get you to your next step? One of the most discouraging situations is to find, after months of planning, that the action didn't get you what you needed. People may feel frustrated, used, impotent, and, as a result, drop out of the organization. The group may find that it now has to deal with the "fallout" of the last action for several months, rather than preparing for the next. Be clear about the *purposes* of your action.

- *What will you get from your action? How do you know?*

- *Is that the direction that you want to go?*

- *Will it get you to the bargaining table? (If that's what you want to happen.)*

2. Are both sides clear on what the fight is about? You should also sit down with your opponent to be sure that you are *fighting about important things.* You may have the right person, but be fighting about the wrong problem.

For example, in the South in the 60s, one group met with the Chief of Police in a town or precinct to demand that his men stop using the word "boy" or "hillbilly" or "broad." The group did not know that the Chief had already issued an order against the use of such words, but his men were not following his order.

The Chief was probably the right person to go to but the problem was incorrect—the problem was not in getting an order written, but in getting the order enforced.

- *What do you see the problem as being?*

- *What does the other side see the problem as being? How do you know?*

- *Have you checked with all reliable sources to be sure you know all aspects of the situation? (Before storming off, are you sure you have all the facts?)*

3. Is the threat believable? It is important to get across to the other side as clearly as possible what will happen if they do not come through on your demands. Spell it out slowly and carefully to them. This is called *making your threat believable.* People act quickly when they are truly threatened. When they think you are just bluffing, they will bluff back.

A good example of a believable threat was when some Japanese railroad workers, who were striking for better pay, chained themselves to the tracks in front of a long freight train. They had some friends put padlocks on the chains which were wrapped around their bodies and the tracks. Then their friends threw the keys into a nearby river. All this was done in full view of the engineers who had broken the strike and were going to drive the trains for the bosses. The trains did not go; the workers got their raises.

You can make your threats just as believable if you go over them in a straightforward and reasonable manner with your opponent.

- *What is your threat?*

- *Will the threat lose your public support or be misinterpreted or manipulated to your disadvantage?*

- *Can you follow through on it?*

- *What kind(s) of risk(s) are involved? Are you prepared?*

4. Will it throw the other side off balance? A good tactic is one which the other side is not expecting, something which takes him out of his usual sphere of operation and places the person in an unfamiliar setting.

One way to do this, as organizer Shel Trapp says, is to "fuse the enemy's public and private world." The lives of elected and corporate leaders are more contradictory than most lives because they are expected to perform "socially responsible duties" while also using their power in traditional dehumanizing ways. For instance, a group of protestors fused President Carter's public and private image when they entered a church where Carter was attending services, and condemned the Carter proposal for a neutron bomb as being un-Christian. Churches, leaders' homes and places the officials frequent are good places to meld public and private worlds.

Another tactic is to show your power when the opposition is least expecting it. When a local city council refused to vote on a housing department for the third consecutive time ("Remember, these things take time," they were constantly told), a citizen group decided, with pillows in hand, to camp out in city hall until the department had been established, because "City Hall is safer than our apartments." A special bill was passed in special session that night.

- *Where is the other side vulnerable?*
- *Can you identify contradictions (exact instances) or hypocracies in what the other side claims to be doing?*
- *How can you make those contradictions known to the public (and believable—remember that the public often sides with authority)?*
- *How can the opposition be caught off-guard?*

5. Will it dramatize the issue? Is it fun? When an issue is dramatized, it is evident even to an outsider why people are upset and want something changed. Dramatization can build membership, and get press.

- *Are there any visual or auditory images your issues brings to mind which can dramatize your point? Can the images be used educationally or humorously? Symbolically?*
- *Are there certain oppressive elements about the issue which can be dramatized in a way which will hit the average citizen?*

Lionel Delevingne

When anti-nuclear groups around the country wanted to warn the public of the dangers of nuclear radiation, they released helium-filled balloons bearing postcards from potential plant sites. The wind-driven balloons traveled in the same direction radiation would travel if there was a leak in a power plant. People up to 100 miles downwind from the sites found the postcards attached to the balloons and returned them with information about where they were found. The event not only reached the media in those cities and towns, it also was an excellent educational tool for those who found the balloons.

Add a little fun to the drama, and watch the membership and press come even more alive. Here are some examples of "fun" type activities:

• When, in one midwestern city, one bank continually red-lined a neighborhood, the neighborhood residents went out to red-line the bank president's home—with paper streamers.

• When a group of tenants became angry that the housing authority had not exterminated cockroaches in tenements, they mailed hundreds of the cockroaches to the housing authority administration building, saying, "Since we are not allowed to have animals here, you will have to take your animals back."

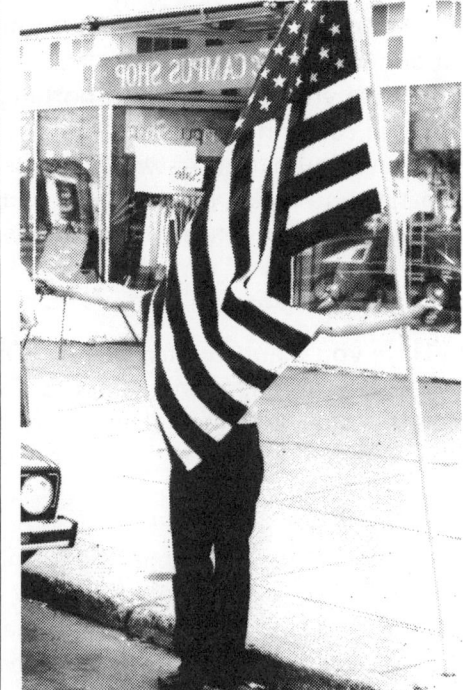
Kayla Kirsch/Jennifer Cobb

Lionel Delevingne

6. Always get the opponent's position in writing. Ask them to write out and sign any promise they make. Sometimes they will say they agree with your demands, but nothing is ever said about when and how they will carry their "agreement" out. Don't leave until this is made clear, and you have it in writing. Also, ask them to sign a copy of the demands you make, because later on they may claim they never talked with you and never heard what you wanted.

• *Do you have the settlement in writing?*

• *Is it reliable and official?*

7. Have you planned alternatives? This is called "contingency," or "what if" planning. What happens if, during a negotiation session, the other side gives in to demands No. 1 and No. 2, but says no to No. 3? What happens if the other side offers an alternative plan?

Alternative strategies are key to an organizing effort, so that even if the circumstances change, the members or spokespeople are prepared as far as possible with a variety of plans to meet the changing circumstances. It is the other side that we want to catch off balance, and keep off balance, not the members of your organization.

• *What possible specific responses could the other side make?*

• *What responses do you have to their responses?*

• *Which responses will work best for you?*

• *Is everyone from your group agreed upon and clear about what alternative strategies would be used and under what circumstances?*

8. Have potential supporters been readied? Community organizations are usually drastically outmatched (resource-wise) by their opponents, and so must rely upon support from other groups for support. It's good to have potential support lined-up, rehearsed and waiting in the wings.

• *Which individuals or groups would most probably support you? Make a large list. If you have trouble coming up with resources, ask yourself:*
  —*Who else would gain from our action?*
  —*Who has resources we could use?*
  —*Who has said they would support us?*
  —*Who has supported us in the past?*
  —*Who has similar values, or claims to have similar values?*

• *Which of these individuals or groups are most accessible? Most powerful?*

THE WIZARD OF ID — By Parker & Hart

9. Is it possible to meet your opponent on your own grounds? (Or at least on neutral territory.) Every time you have to go to him, sit in his office, wait for him to answer his phone, it puts you at a psychological disadvantage.

• *Can you determine the site of the negotiation or meeting?*

• *If so, what site would be best for you?*

10. Do you need to practice before you act? (See Collaborative Strategies, Question 7.)

11. Have you underestimated who you are working with? (See Campaign Strategies, Question 5.)

12. Are you ready internally? (See Collaborative Strategies, Question 6.)

•*Who should be there?*

•*What times of day put you at the advantage?*

TACTICS IN ORGANIZING
(From Saul Alinsky)

"We will either find a way or make one."
—Hanibal

"Tactics" means doing what you can with what you have. Saul Alinsky lists a number of ways to do those things:

Rule 1: Power is not only what you have but what the enemy thinks you have.

Rule 2: Never go outside the experience of your people.

Rule 3: Wherever possible, go outside the experience of the enemy.

Rule 4: Make the enemy live up to their own book of rules.

Rule 5: Ridicule is your best and most potent weapon.

Rule 6: A good tactic is one that your people enjoy. If your people are not having a ball doing it, there is something very wrong with the tactic.

Rule 7: A tactic that drags on too long becomes a drag. People can sustain militant interest in any issue for only a limited time, after which it becomes a ritualistic commitment, like going to church on Sunday mornings. New issues and crises are always developing, and one's reaction becomes, "Well, my heart bleeds for all those people and I am all for the boycott, but after all there are other important things in life."

Rule 8: Keep the pressure on with different tactics and actions and utilize all events of the period for your purpose.

Rule 9: The threat is usually more terrifying than the thing itself.

Rule 10: The major premise for tactics is the development of operations that will maintain a constant pressure upon the opposition. It is this unceasing pressure that results in the reactions from the opposition that are essential for the success of the campaign. It should be remembered not only that the **action is in the reaction** but that **action is itself a consequence of reaction** and of reaction to the reaction, *ad infinitum*. The pressure produces the reaction, and constant pressure sustains action.

Rule 11: If you push a negative hard and deep enough it will break through its counterside.

Rule 12: The price of a successful attack is a constructive alternative. You cannot risk being trapped by the enemy in his sudden agreement with your demand and saying, "You're right—we don't know what to do about this issue. Now you tell us."

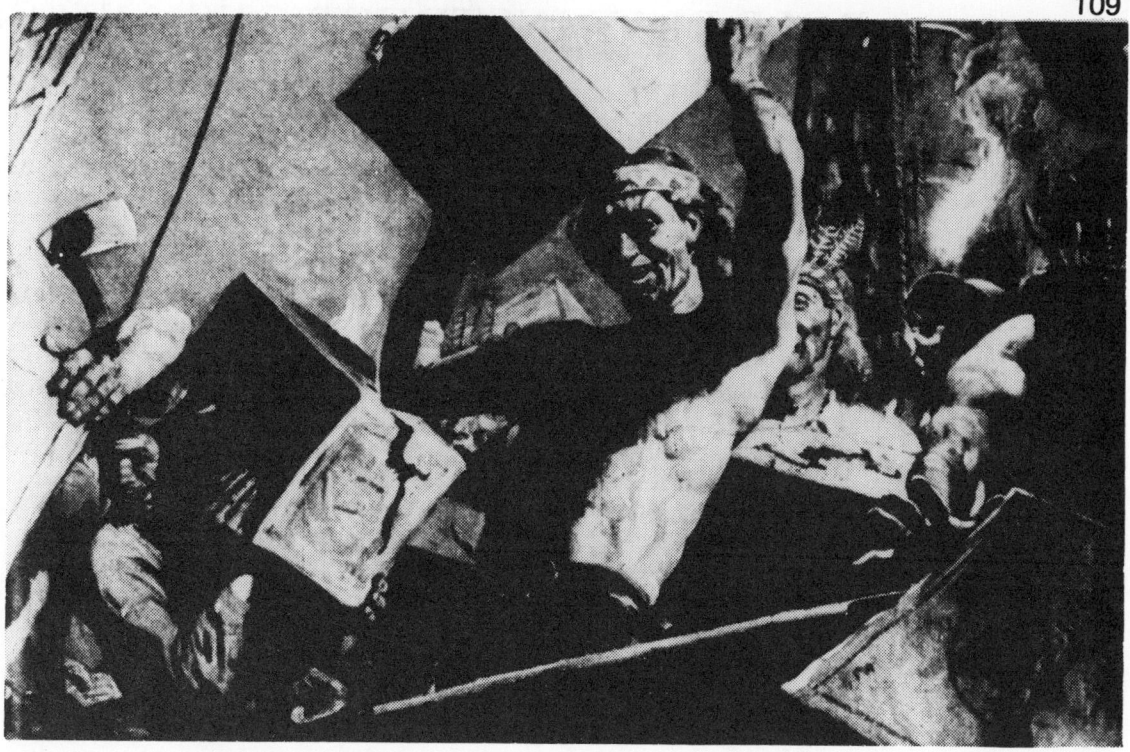

ROLE-PLAYING: A "Rehearsal" for Action

Role-playing provides participants with the chance to act out practice-organizing. It is fun, high energy, and provides people with data on themselves.

Two role-plays are provided here. Both allow participants to practice the community organizing process. The first is called "Holyspring" (which was done for residents of Holyoke and Springfield, Mass.), and it allows participants to practice what it feels like to be organized, as well as concentrating on the need to negotiate.

I like to interrupt the role-play once during Step 4 and ask participants to think about how they are approaching people, and think of perhaps planning a more productive approach.

The "Frankshire County" scenario was written around specific needs of a client group from Franklin and Berkshire Counties in Massachusettts. It allows people to practice the same type of concerns as the "Holyspring" example but emphasizes the work of the community organizers in the process.

At least three people are allowed to be community organizers in this role-play. I suggest you may want to stop action periodically and ask the organizers how they feel about what they are doing; maybe ask the "community people" to do the same; and offer the organizers some suggestions as to how they can be more effective.

Note that both options deal with very specific economic, as well as social service and community issues. The attempt here was to allow people to think in terms of dealing with root causes, and see coalitions as an important, and useful strategy.

These role-plays can be used to generate data to which the specific exercises in the manual can then be applied. If these role-plays are not particularly relevant to you, why not design your own?

ROLE-PLAY INSTRUCTIONS AND SCHEDULE

You are one of the players in this simulation. Read through all of the material in this packet, then follow the schedule shown below.

The players are residents of one of five wards. Each ward will meet together to communicate role information and discuss strategies. After these initial meetings, informal lobbying of other individual Council and ward members by various players will begin. A formal meeting of the City Council will follow. The first part of the meeting will consist of statements delivered by the ward representatives, either supporting or opposing the resolution. After brief discussion all councilors will vote on this question. The vote of the councilors will end the simulation.

The OBJECTIVE of the game is to lobby the councilors and other ward groups to effectively represent your point of view regarding the union resolution. The success of your efforts will be determined by the vote.

1
Players receive packets and read instructions and other material.
(5 min.)

2
Players meet in their ward group to discuss the groups' position, goal and strategies.
(10 min.)

3
Players informally lobby other Councilors and ward groups and prepare statements.
(30-45 min.)

4
Municipal Council Meeting: statements and discussion.
(15 min.)

5
Vote by all Councilors.
(5 min.)
End simulation.

Holyspring is a small city (pop. 30,000) located in Western Massachusetts. Once a significant textile and paper processing center, Holyspring now suffers serious financial problems, as several industries have moved south and overseas primarily because of cheap labor. The results for Holyspring are high unemployment and an eroding tax base.

Presently another industry, Tootleoo Textiles, is threatening to relocate in Atlanta, Georgia, unless it can receive a 50% tax abatement from the city and freeze union wages at the current rate. Workers at local 008, feeling that to strike would be futile, are themselves interested in purchasing the plant but would do so only if the city were to underwrite and pay interest on a commercial loan for them.

The major decision-making body of Holyspring is the City Council, made up of councilors elected by each of the five wards of the city. The chairperson of the Council has received a petition for a resolution to have the city underwrite and pay interest on a loan to be taken out by the local union. A meeting of the City Council has been called to hear the opinions of the different wards and to vote on this issue. The chairperson has sent letters on this subject to all councilors, and some councilors have discussed the problem with people in their wards and have begun to express opposition or support on the resolution. Councilors representing some other wards have not yet stated their point of view. At the meeting, a representative from each of the five wards will express their point of view and then all councilors will vote on whether or not to pass the resolution. The majority will decide. Each councilor will vote according to what she feels is in the best interest of her ward and will take into account the wishes of ward citizens and the arguments made during the presentations to the Council.

ROLE-PLAY SCENARIO #1

The five wards and their positions on the resolution at the first public notification include:

- **Ward A:** a well-to-do neighborhood of professionals (appears to be against the resolution).

- **Ward B:** where the chairperson resides, a low- to middle-income area near the plant (appears to favor the resolution).

- **Ward C:** a low-income area in which the plant is located (appears to be in favor of the resolution).

- **Ward D:** a well-to-do neighborhood (appears to be against the resolution).

- **Ward E:** a combination low- to middle-income residential neighborhood and the business section of the city (has not taken a stand as a ward on the issue).

WARD A DESCRIPTION

Ward A consists of well-to-do professional and business people, relatively conservative in their point of view. They are strongly against the resolution, believing that the workers are not competent to run the plant, that the resolution smacks of socialism, that the unions are to blame for high wages and non-productivity and as a result management has decided to pull out of the city. The residents here feel that if the town is to spend money on anything, it should spend money on improving a zoo and park area in Ward A, to make sure that the well-to-do taxpayers do not move out of the city.

The central goal of Ward A residents and their councilor is to ensure that the City Council does not pass the resolution. In order to attain this goal, the councilors of Ward A must organize effectively to defeat the resolution, bringing influence to bear on other wards and individuals, and present their views at the City Council meeting.

WARD B DESCRIPTION

Ward B consists of low- and middle-income families, and appears to be for the proposal, primarily because many families would be negatively affected by the plant's closing. Some residents are also concerned that small grocery stores, bars and restaurants lose customers with the plant's closing. The only substantial support against the resolution comes from a few factory workers who are looking forward to jobs in Atlanta, where the factory is planning to move.

The Ward B councilor is the chairperson of the Council. The central goal of the Ward B councilor and most of the ward residents is to insure that the City Council passes the resolution. In order to attain this goal, the residents of Ward B must organize effectively to pass the resolution, bringing influence to bear on the other ward groups and individuals, and present their views at the City Council meeting.

WARD C DESCRIPTION

Ward C is the lowest income ward in the city. It is the ward where the plant may be closed. The ward is in strong support of the resolution because many residents are employed by the plant, and plant employees support many local businesses in the area.

The central goal of the Ward C residents and council is to insure that the City Council passes the resolution. In order to attain this goal, the residents of Ward C must organize effectively to pass the resolution, bringing influence to bear on other ward groups and individuals, and present their views at the City Council meeting.

WARD D DESCRIPTION

Ward D is a well-to-do, liberal section of the city. The ward appears to oppose the proposal because the residents have been upset about the air and water pollution the factory causes in the ward, and because ward residents feel that workers are not really capable of running their own plant. The only substantial support for the proposal comes from a few people who feel that high unemployment will increase vandalism, theft and other crime in the area.

The central goal of the Ward D councilor and most of the ward residents is to insure that the City Council does not pass the resolution. In order to attain this goal, the councilor of Ward D must organize effectively to defeat the resolution, bringing influence to bear on other ward groups and individuals, and present their views at the City Council meeting.

WARD E DESCRIPTION

Ward E borders the factory, includes both residential and the downtown business district of the city. At this point, Ward E residents and its Councilor are unclear as to what stand they will take. Some employees of the factory live in the residential part of the ward and want to see it remain; on the other hand, there are those residents who empathize with the ward member who said, "Things may be bad now, but at least we know what we've got."

Business in the area is equally divided. It does not want to see unemployment, but also does not want to see untested projects fall apart.

ROLE-PLAY TASKS: ALL WARDS EXCEPT WARD E

1. The following tasks should be accomplished during your **first ward group meeting**:

   • Clarify the ward group position in regard to the resolution.

   • Identify target groups, i.e., those groups or individuals outside your own whose support you wish to enlist and decide what strategies you will use to get their support.

   • Identify linkage groups, i.e., groups holding similar interests with which you may want to form coalitions and decide what strategies you will use.

   • Prepare or assign someone to prepare a four minute speech to the Municipal Council meeting presenting your ward group position.

2. The following tasks should be accomplished during the **influence/lobbying period** of the simulation:

   • Contact target groups and individuals and implement strategies to gain their support.

   • Contact linkage groups and implement strategies for the formation of coalitions.

3. The following tasks should be accomplished during the **Municipal Council meeting**:

   • A spokesperson from your ward group should present a statement of the group's views to the meeting.

WARD E TASKS

1. During your **first group meeting** you should clarify the group position in regard to the resolution and decide what strategies you will use to get additional information and hear arguments for and against the increase.

2. During the **influence/lobbying period** of the simulation you should implement strategies of information-gathering, hear relevant arguments and meet as a group again to decide what stand Ward E councilors will take on the resolution.

3. If appropriate, Ward E should present its views to the **Municipal Council meeting** through a four-minute statement by a group spokesperson.

ROLE-PLAY SCENARIO #2

Frankshire County is a large, rural low-income county located in northwestern Massachusetts. Once known as the home of several major paper and textile companies, the county now suffers serious financial and social problems as several industries have moved south and overseas, primarily because of cheaper labor. The results for Frankshire County are high unemployment, an eroding tax base and a lack of adequate social services.

One noticeable result of the lack of strong economic base has been the decline in health among many of the County's residents. Hospitals have noticed a distinct increase in measles and mumps; home-care agencies have not been able to receive adequate treatment for an increasing elderly population. In a recent health study, the regional Health Planning Council has stated that the two major problems of the county are the need for increased accessibility for primary medical services, and the overall high cost of health care.

In part due to the increased health care problems, the local B agency has received funds for three CETA workers to help residents of the three major areas of the county organize for better services.

One of the three organizers, the one from the western part of the county, has come up with a plan. She would propose that the county take $280,000 out of the county budget to set up a non-profit health clinic that would provide free immunizations, and other medical services on a sliding scale. The money would be used as seed money for two years until the center would receive a certificate of need so that it could receive third party payments, thus becoming self-sufficient.

Fortunately or unfortunately for the organizer, (you decide) her idea has received some notoriety, for she is suggesting that the $280,000 be taken from $300,000 ear-marked to repair the county road that leads to the Tooteloo Tool and Textile Company, the county's leading employer. Some management leaders, feeling that this is just another example of ways that the area has not supported industry, are pressuring the county not to abandon the road monies. There is a rumor that if the county does not provide for the road, "Tooteloo might just tooteloo away."

The County Commissioner's have decided to make a decision on the next year's budget on October 9, 1977.

Now design your own instructions, schedule and tasks to implement this role-play scenario, using the Holyspring material as a model. Good luck!

Lionel Delevingne

CHAPTER V:
EVALUATION AND FUTURE DIRECTIONS

Since organizing is an on-going process of actions, the results of individual actions must be evaluated. Evaluation allows people to figure out what has happened, as a guide to future actions.

Evaluation can be done both informally and formally. Informal evaluation allows people to *feel* what they have done. Formal evaluation allows people to *think about* what they have done. Both processes are important.

Many people use the time immediately after a meeting, event or other action to evaluate informally. Let's say that a group has just had a major meeting with the mayor. The action was something that had taken several weeks of planning, and the mayor finally agreed to policy changes that the group had been fighting for. The group might want to go out for beers (carrot juice, root beer, or what have you) to talk about what happened, express feelings and celebrate. This should be encouraged for several reasons:

• it allows people to express immediate reactions to what has just happened;

it allows people to share perceptions of what has happened;

• it allows the group to clarify situations that may need clarifying;

• it encourages friendliness as people "let their hair down," and step out of roles they may have assumed within the organization;

• it helps build solidarity as people re-live a situation they've been through together;

• it allows people to begin to talk about what they want to do in the future.

But this evaluation probably won't be enough. You should want the full impact of the planning and the action to settle in before you really begin to evaluate what you've done. So at a meeting at least three or four days after your event, you should ask the group the following questions:

- *How do we **feel** about what happened (not **think**, but **feel**)?*

- *Are we clear about what happened?*

- *What were the results of what happened?*

- *Did it get us where we wanted to go? Were we successful?*

- *If not, what could we have done differently?*

- *Are there certain people we should talk to who could provide us with more objective information about how successful we were?*

- *What did we learn in all this about ourselves individually? about the organization? about the system?*

- *What is the next step? Why? When? Where? How?*

Newsletters:

Acorn News
523 West 15th St.
Little Rock, Ark.
72202

Disclosure
c/o NTIC
1123 W. Washington Blvd.
Chicago, Ill.
60610

Humanizing City Life
Box 303
Worthington, Ohio
43085

People and Taxes
P.O. Box 14198
Washington, D.C.
20044

Beacon Hill Update
(Monitors State House activities affecting low-income people)
Room 744
294 Washington Street
Boston, Mass.
02108

Self-Reliance
c/o Institute for Local Self Reliance
1717 18th St., NW
Washington, D.C.
20009

New Unity Newspaper
(Labor and community newspaper, Western Mass.)
Box 891
Springfield, Mass.
01101

Haymarket News
Haymarket Peoples Fund
2 Holyoke St.
Cambridge, Mass.
02138

Resist
(A Call To Resist Illegitimate Authority)
324 Somerville Ave.
Somerville, Mass.
02143

Just Economics
1735 T Street, NW
Washington, D.C.
20009

The Fair Fighter
Mass Fair Share
364 Boylston St.
Boston, Mass.
02116

NETCCOmmunications
New England Training Center for Community Organizers
19 Davis St.
Providence, R.I.
02908

Peacework
(Newsletter of New England Chapter of American Friends Service Committee)
c/o AFSC
2161 Massachusetts Ave.
Cambridge, Mass.
02140

Films:

American Friends Service Committee
160 No. 15th St.
Philadelphia, Pa.
19102

American Friends Service Committee provides films and slide tapes on many important social issues. It is often possible to contact AFSC and have a speaker come and show films or slides and lead discussions. AFSC should be considered a resource for any group going about social change. Their brochure lists films that deal with imperialism, racism, war/peace, etc.

C.C. Films Catalog
Communication Commission
National Council of the Churches of Christ
Room 860
475 Riverside Dr.
New York, N.Y.
10027
(212) 870-2541

Approximately 30 films dealing with justice and liberation (**Last Grave at Dimbaza; Bottle Babies**); migrant workers, Appalachia, and the black experience, ethical and moral issues (amnesty, drug addiction, education, environment, global consciousness, etc.) are listed in this catalog. Films sell from $160 to $600.

Films of Social Comment
Contemporary and McGraw-Hill Films
McGraw-Hill Book Company
330 West 42nd St.
New York, N.Y.
10036

RE: SOURCES

Over 60 films for rent (beginning at $6) or sale ($75 and up) are listed. The brochure lists the following categories: Feature Documentary; War and Peace; Social Problems; Intergroup Relations; Poverty; Problems of Employment; Education and Guidance; International Understanding and Cooperation.

Besides their brochure, McGraw-Hill also has a newsletter of films (annotated) called Contemporary Newsletter, 1221 Avenue of the Americas, New York, N.Y. 10020.

Green Mountain Post Films
P.O. Box 177
Montague, Mass.
01351
(413) 863-4754

Green Mountain Post Films both produces and distributes films. Their major emphasis is on anti-nuclear information, a natural sub-

ject for one of the members of the film company, Sam Lovejoy. Included in the 1978 edition of the catalog are such anti-nuclear films as **Lovejoy's Nuclear War, The Last Resort** (both award winning films produced by GMP), **More Nuclear Power Stations, Better Active Today Than Radioactive Tomorrow, Nuclear Reaction in Wyhl.** Other films include **Union Maids** (women organizing), **Different Times, Different Places** (a sympathetic look at a farm for the mentally retarded) and **Living the Good Life** (about back-to-earth-ers Helen and Scott Nearing). Films can be rented on a sliding scale (beginning at about $35) or sold. Write for catalog.

New Day Films
Box 315
Franklin Lakes, N.J.
07417

New Day Films began as a women's film distribution co-op. They now handle a number of educational films which treat a wide range of human issues.

Impact Films Catalog
144 Bleeker Street
New York, N.Y.
10012
(212) 924-1652

This catalog lists over 100 films for rent, all professionally well done, in such areas as justice, (CBS's **Justice in America; Justice Delayed, Justice Denied: Justice and the Poor**); domestic issues (poverty, union organizing, welfare rights, housing, Native American issues); ecology (including films on nuclear power, pollution, socialized medicine, black perspectives, women's studies, Africa, Latin America, Ireland, Indo-China, war, peace and fascism. Films are on a rental basis, most under $50.

New England Training Center for Community Organizers (NETCCO)
19 Davis St.
Providence, R.I.
02908

NETCCO has video-tapes available for the cost of shipping only. Tapes include: **Community Congress Workshop; Neighborhoods First; Coalitions; New Territory; Community Development Corporations and Community Organizing; American Nightmare; PACE Congress.**

STAR Films
(A Peoples' Film Library)
2 Holyoke St.
Cambridge, Mass.
02138
(413)
(617) 661-3007

This is a radical film library. The 40 or so films that are available through STAR films can be rented for between $5 and $10, making them (intentionally) very accessible to community groups that have no money. Films listed in their catalog include films that deal with sexism, Latin America **Attica**, and two films about the struggles of neighborhood groups to save their housing and communities in the face of absentee landlords. Other films include **East of the Earth** and **Potemkin**.

Books:

Blaming the Victim
William Ryan
Bantam Paperback
New York, 1974

This book powerfully details how our culture, and more specifically, our human service system is designed to blame the victims of poverty rather than to confront the real villians, class and race.

Choosing a Tactic
Steve Max
Midwest Academy
600 W. Fullerton
Chicago, Ill. 60614

This 25 page manual evaluates tactics commonly used by direct action community organizations. Tactics evaluated include: actions, elections, law suits, education, service and strikes. Extremely helpful material by staff of one of the best known training centers in the country.

The Community Development Process
William and Loureide Biddle

A good primer for organizers, and overview of the potential for community organization and development.

Community Organization: Theory, Principles and Practice
Murry G. Ross
Harper and Row, 1967

A good basic community organization manual...used internationally.

Creating the Future: A Guide for Living and

Working for Social Change
Charles Bietz and Michael Washburn
Bantam Paperback
New York, 1974

Provides strategies and approaches written to get to the roots of social problems (resources contributed by Vocations for Social Change). The book discusses choosing a social change vocation, given strategies for building community in a number of social fields; gives particularly helpful insight and political philosophy for those who are feeling burned-out.

Creating Social Change
Gerald Zaltman, Phillip Kotler and Ira Kaufman
Holt Rinehart and Winston
New York, 1972

Almost 700 pages of social change theories, strategies and issues; browse through before purchasing.

Direct Action and Liberal Democracy
April Carter
Harper and Row, 1973

Written on the premise that significant social change has come only from direct action, this book uses the women's and trade union movements in Britain and the Civil Rights movement in the United States to examine which methods of direct action work, and why those methods work.

Encouraging Community Development
William and Loureide Biddle

A follow-up on their book, **Community Development Process**, written especially for para-professionals and those who work with them.

**An End to Hierarchy!
An End to Competition!
Organizing the Politics and Economics of Survival
Frederick C. Thayer**

This book calls for an end to hierarchical and competitive structures (which go hand-in-hand with each other), and claims that it is possible, easy to do, and the only way to abandon alienation; provides interesting discussion on structure in organizing.

**Finding Community: A Guide to Community Research and Action
W. Ron Jones
James E. Freel and Associates
Palo Alto California
1971**

This book is divided into 11 chapters, each chapter dealing with a specific problem faced by most communities (food costs, welfare, health, housing, etc.). Each chapter is divided into indictments (what's wrong in each area), brief readings, some methods for community research and action (including success models) and offering alternatives. Good reading for community groups.

**From Poverty to Dignity
Charles Hampden Turner**

This is a well thought out social and psychological case for the Community Development Corporations as a major weapon in the fight against poverty. Slow but powerful reading.

**Hang-Ups: Some Common Problems of People Who Organize Other People Into Communities
Alan McSurely
Organizers' Library Service of the Southern Conference Educational Fund
Louisville, Ky.**

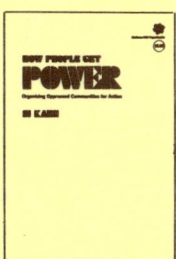

**How People Get Power: Organizing Oppressed Communities for Action
Si Kahn
McGraw Hill
1970**

One of the better-known organizers of poor communities has written a step-by-step (from the time the organizer enters a community to do research, to the time the organizer leaves, confident that the community group can go it along) organizing manual, chock full of techniques and tactics.

**Neighborhood Government: The Local Foundations of Political Life
Milton Kotler
Bobbs-Merrill Co.
1969**

This book provides a history of how local neighborhoods lost their power to downtown and big-business interests, and provides some possible methods to regain that power. a forerunner of appropriate technology for the local neighborhood...strong argument for local control.

**Neighborhood Power, The New Localism: Returning Political and Economic Power To Community Life
David Morris and Karl Hess
Beacon Paperback
New York, 1975**

This book uses successes around the country to show how a self-sufficient community moves from the initial stages of community awareness and organization to the creation of service networks (co-ops, clinics, tenant unions), to the development of community-sustaining funds, which serve as seed money for other collective enterprises, and finally to the rise of neighborhood self-government. This book is a must for community workers.

**The New Socialist Revolution
Michael P. Lerner
Dell Publishing
New York, 1973**

A helpful, theoretical analysis of social and economic problems in the country, and discussion of what strategies exist to deal with those problems.

**Pedagogy of the Oppressed
Paulo Freire
Herter
New York, 1970**

In this famous work, Freire uncovers the oppressive nature of almost all educational practice as presently conceived; difficult reading, but well worth the effort.

**People Power: An Alternative to 1984
Morgan J. Doughton
MediaAmerica
Bethlehem, Pa., 1976**

Gives innumerable examples of how people overcome bureaucratic structures and solve community problems without outside help.

**The Politicized Economy
Michael Best and Michael Connally**

At last, a brief, easy to understand analysis of economic roots of today's social problems. If organizers don't deal with issues raised in this book, we may be organizing for band-aid solutions forever.

**The Politics of Turmoil: Poverty, Race, and the Urban Crisis
Frances Fox Piven and Richard Cloward
Vintage Paperback
New York, 1972**

A series of articles that radically questions liberal strategies for social change, and strongly advocates for confrontation politics.

**Politics of Nonviolent Action
Gene Sharpe**

This three-volume set is the most comprehensive work yet on non-violent action as an organizing strategy. The set deals with the theory of non-violent action (Volume I); the methods of non-violent action, including 198 historically documented examples (Volume II); and preparing and conducting non-violent action (Volume III).

Books (cont'd)

Poor Peoples' Movements: Why They Succeed, How They Fail
Frances Fox Piven and Richard Cloward
Pantheon Books
New York, 1977

This could be one of the most important books written on organizing. The book analyzes four social movements of the 20th Century: the Unemployed Workers movement, the Industrial Workers' Movement, the Civil Rights Movement, and the Welfare Rights Movement, destroying a lot of myths about how successful those movements were. The book is very precise about how the authors feel power is generated and used in America, what organizers have done in the past, and what the establishments have done about organizers' actions. The authors are also quite exact about what actions movements should take in the future.

Power Inc.
Morton Mintz and Jerry S. Cohen
Bantam Books
New York, 1977

Nearly 800 well-documented pages of who runs America, and how they run it—exposes government and corporate power elite. Categories include government and corporate secrecy, conflicts of interest, lack of accountability, and implications for citizens.

The Psychology of Social Movements
Hadley Cantril
Science Editions
New York

A social psychologist takes a look at social movements of the first half of this century and deals with the questions of what motivates people to follow untried leaders, what social environment does to make people susceptible, and what people are thinking about when they "lose themselves" in a social cause.

A Public Citizen's Action Manual
Donald K. Ross

Part of the Nader family of books, this manual includes "how-to" information in such areas as consumerism, employment and employment discrimination, taxes, government responsiveness, organizing citizen action groups. Other Nader family books relevant to organizing include: **Action for a Change, The Company State, Corporate Power in America, The Politics of Land,** and **Whistle-Blowing.**

Regulating the Poor
Frances Fox and Richard Cloward
Vintage Paperback
New York, 1972

Explores the history of welfare and social services from the 16th Century to the War on Poverty program; excellent analysis of how the powerful use and manipulate social services and well worth reading for those in the helping professions who want to understand this profession's roots and dilemmas.

Reveille for Radicals
Saul D. Alinsky
Vintage Paperback
New York

Written for the most part while Alinsky was in jail during the Chicago organizing days of the 30s, this book is chock full of organizing ideas and strategies.

The Rich Get Richer and The Rest Pay Taxes
Massachusetts Public Finance Project
1975

An excellent analysis of the state and local tax structure in Massachusetts (or is it Taxachusetts)—who wins (and how much they win) and who loses (and how much we lose).

Rules for Radicals: A Practical Primer for Realistic Radicals
Saul D. Alinsky
Vintage Paperbacks
New York, 1971

A must for organizers, the topics include: tactics, purposes, educating the organizer; written by the granddaddy of community organizers.

Small Is Beautiful: Economics as is People Mattered
E. F. Schumacher
Harper and Row
New York, 1973

If you are interested in community economics, you should read this book by the person who more than anyone else is responsible for the rise in interest in alternative economics and appropriate technology.

Social Conflicts and Social Movements
Anthony Oberschall
Prentice Hall
1973

If you read this book, you'll be picking the brains of a good social historian. Most of this material is not used by organizers, but should be...the book explores the causes of social conflicts, formation of conflict groups and social movements; participants in oppression movements; the role of leaders and activists; the formation and spread of ideologies; confrontation; mechanisms of social control; the process of conflict regulation.

Socialism and Revolution
Andre Gorz

Outlines in broad terms a strategy for bringing about socialism in a capitalist economy: who one works with, pacing, style and structures of organizing. Gorz is one of the most important theorists of the Left.

The Soft Revolution: A Student Handbook for Turning Schools Around
Neil Postman and Charles Weingarten
Delacorte Press
New York, 1971

While written primarily for those interested in changing schools, the book provides some excellent ways to strategize around issues. See especially pages 3-12 concerning the use of the "judo approach to social change." Also filled with quickie ideas and success models.

Some ABC's of Community Organization: Organizing Groups and Individuals for Effective Local Action
Ronnie M. Moore
Afram Assoc.
Harlem, New York
1972

Strategy for a Living Revolution
George Lakey

Lakey provides a global analysis of political/economic/environmental problems, and a step-by-step strategy to deal with these problems. Historically well documented, the book discusses such problems as nationalism, and the conflicts between regional large scale planning and local control in bringing about social change.

Studying Your Community
Roland Warren
Free Press
MacMillan and Co.
1955

Although over 20 years old, the book is extremely relevant in helping organizers research education, political structures, economic and social service structures in various communities.

Truth, Love, and Social Change and Other Essays on Social Change
Roland Warren
MacMillan and Co.
1972

The first section, "Strategies of Change," is well worth consideration of any organizer.

Up With The Ranks: How Community Organizers Develop Community Leadership
Mark Lindberg
NETCCO
19 Davis, Providence, R.I.
1977

A handy, common sense, easy to read and understand manual, describing a process of building grass-roots leadership in a community.

Urban Disinvestment: New Implications for Community Organization Research and Public Policy
Available through the National Center for Urban and Ethnic Affairs Division
National Training and Information Center
(see Training Centers .)

Why Organizers Fail: The Story of a Rent Strike
Harry Brill
University of California Press
1971

This is a first-hand account of the behavior of a group of militant organizers during a 14 month public housing rent strike. The rent strike, according to the author, illustrates a political dilemma confronting poor: to win a major reform from a formidable and often unyielding establishment requires building effective political organization; yet when the poor do act in concert, it is often to their own disadvantage.

Where It's At: A Research Guide for Community Organizing
Jill Hamberg
New England Free Press
791 Tremont St.
Boston, Ma.
1967

Handbooks:

The Children's Yellow Pages
Holyoke-Chicopee Council for Children
276 High St.
Holyoke, Ma. 01040
1976
$1

The first comprehensive resource manual for children's services; can be used as a guide to what citizens can do to improve the quality of life for children, as well as an analysis of children's services and as a model for community organizing. It attempts to take a look at economic and political reasons why many children suffer as they do; also provides hundreds of resources in the Holyoke-Springfield area.

Community Organizing Handbook
ACORN
523 W. 15th St.
Little Rock, Ark. 72202
$3

This manual is written by and is, in many cases, about ACORN— one of the most effective organizing projects in the history of community organizing.

Resource Manual for a Living Revolution
Virginia Coover, Ellen Deacon, Charles Easer, Christopher Moore
New Society Press
Movement for a New Society
4722 Baltimore Ave.
Philadelphia, Pa. 19143
$4

Over 300 pages of theories, strategies and workshop ideas are listed in this manual, put out by members of Movement for a New Society. Sections include: the theoretical basis for change; working in groups; developing communities of support; personal growth; consciousness-raising; training and education; organizing for change; exercises and other tools.